SAUDI ARABIA

PAUL AARTS
CAROLIEN ROELANTS

Saudi Arabia

A Kingdom in Peril

HURST & COMPANY, LONDON

First published in the United Kingdom in 2015 by
C. Hurst & Co. (Publishers) Ltd.,
41 Great Russell Street, London, WC1B 3PL
© Carolien Roelants and Paul Aarts, 2015, and originally published as
Saoedi-Arabië. De revolutie die nog moet komen,
Nieuw Amsterdam Uitgevers, Amsterdam 2013
Revised and updated English translation from Dutch © Donald Gardner, 2015
All rights reserved.
Printed in India

Distributed in the United States, Canada and Latin America by
Oxford University Press, 198 Madison Avenue, New York, NY 10016,
United States of America

A Cataloguing-in-Publication data record for this book
is available from the British Library.

ISBN: 978-1-84904-465-3

This book is printed using paper from registered sustainable
and managed sources.

www.hurstpublishers.com

This book was published with the support of the Dutch Foundation
for Literature

CONTENTS

GENERAL NOTE

Saudis—or others—whose words are quoted in this book were either interviewed by one or other of the authors during their visits to Saudi Arabia or their Twitter posts are quoted. In every other case the source is mentioned in the notes.

The spelling of Arabic names and concepts is in compliance with the Hurst house style. It is worth mentioning the difference between 'al' and 'Al'. The former, followed by a hyphen, is a definite article; the second, with a capital 'A' and without a hyphen, means 'family' or 'house of'.

Just before going to press King Salman announced several important changes in the order of succession and in his government. Clearly the most dramatic change was (according to the announcement) the voluntary departure of Prince Muqrin bin Abd al-Aziz Al Saud as crown prince, followed by the nomination of Prince Muhammad bin Nayef Al Saud ('MbN') in his place. Another important shift was the promotion of the young Prince Muhammad bin Salman Al Saud ('MbS'), who became deputy crown prince. Now most power under the king rests in the hands of these two princes, who preside over committees in the cabinet determining security issues and economic and social development, apart from their functions as minister of interior (MbN) and defense (MbS).

In particular the rise of Muhammad bin Salman has been amazing; his recent appointment came only three months after he had been appointed both minister of defense and chief of his father's court. In this last function he now has been replaced. Will he try to sideline Muhammad bin Nayef, to succeed his father? A power struggle seems to be in the air.

GENERAL NOTE

It was not possible to include these and other changes in the Saudi top in this book. However, they do not undermine our analysis of the present state of affairs at the Royal Court.

ACKNOWLEDGEMENTS

Our grateful thanks are due to Bregje Galema. She has followed Arab-language Twitter posts for many months and made them available to us. It has enriched the material enormously. In the early stages of the book Timo van Dun was of valuable assistance. Finally, Amer Al-Alim gave the entire manuscript a critical reading.

GLOSSARY

Marja-al taqlid   Literally, 'source of emulation'. For Shiites, the high-
                    est religious authority to whom they owe obedience.
                    Believers are free in their choice of *marja*. The title is
                    usually reserved for the highest clerics, holding the
                    rank of 'ayatollah al-ozma' ('highest sign of God' or
                    'grand ayatollah'). Most Shiites in Saudi Arabia fol-
                    low Grand Ayatollah Ali al-Sistani in Najaf (Iraq) as
                    their *marja*.

Mutawwa   In the West known as 'religious police', in Saudi
                    Arabia as *hay'a* (committee). It is the executive arm of
                    the 'Committee for the Promotion of Virtue and
                    Prohibition of Vice'. The force consists of some
                    3,500 agents and thousands of volunteers who oper-
                    ate in the public space to supervise compliance with
                    the rules of sharia.

Sahwa   In general the term means 'awakening', but in the
                    context of Saudi Arabia it alludes specifically to the
                    reform movement that emerged in the 1980s. Its
                    leaders included figures such as Salman al-Awda and
                    Safar al-Hawali.

Salafism   Movement inspired by the first generation of
                    Muslims from the early days of Islam (the period of
                    the *salafiyya*, the ancestors). Supporters advocate a
                    literal interpretation of the Quran and the Hadith

xi

	(traditions)—as the only authoritative sources. There is a wide spectrum of Salafist groups, ranging from apolitical ones to others that are jihadist. Contemporary Salafism originates in Saudi Arabia (see Wahhabism) where it is the state religion.
Shiite, Shiites	Minority tendency in Islam, roughly 10 per cent of all Muslims. They claim that Muhammad's son-in-law, Ali, and his descendants are the rightful successors. The 'Twelver Shiites' (Imamiyya) form the largest group in Saudi Arabia, followed by the Zaidiyyah or 'Fiver Shiites' and the Ismailis or 'Sevener Shiites'.
Sunni, Sunnites	The main tendency in Islam. *Sunna* is Arabic for tradition. Sunni Muslims follow the tradition based on the life of the Prophet Muhammad and his companions. About 90 per cent of the 1.5 billion Muslims worldwide call themselves Sunnis. Of the indigenous Saudi population (roughly 21 million) 85 to 90 per cent are Sunnis and 10 to 15 per cent are Shiites.
Ulama	Religious Scholars.
Wahhabism	A puritan reform movement, founded by Muhammad Ibn Abd al-Wahhab (1703–92), which strives for a return to the ideal society of the first generation of Muslims. They struggle against infidels and idol worship and are anti-Shiite. In 1744 Ibn Abd al-Wahhab formed an alliance with the ruler at the time, Muhammad Ibn Saud. It is an alliance that has survived to this day. The followers of Wahhabism want to avoid all appearance that they worship Ibn Abd al-Wahhab and therefore prefer to call themselves *al-muwahiddun* (those who believe in the oneness of God) or Salafists. Though highly influential, Wahhabis form a minority among Sunni Muslims in Saudi Arabia.

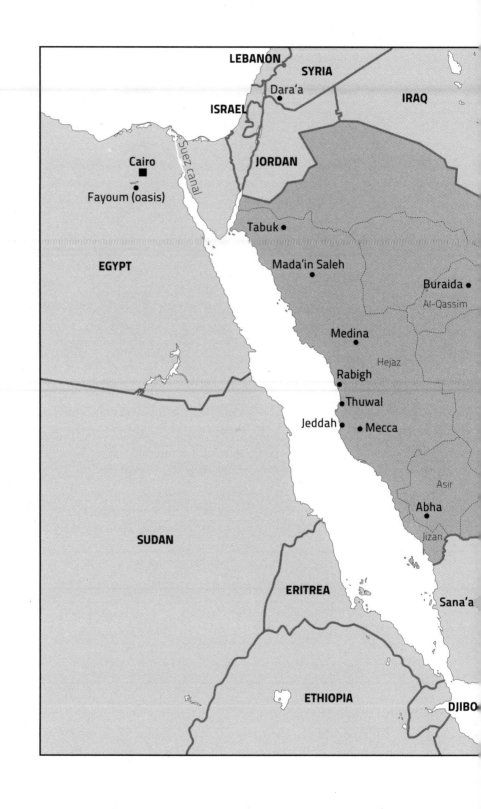

The Saudi Royal family

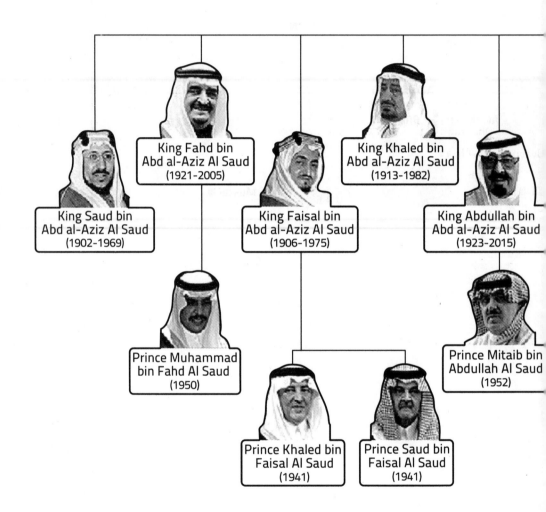

King Saud bin Abd al-Aziz Al Saud (1902-1969)

King Fahd bin Abd al-Aziz Al Saud (1921-2005)

King Faisal bin Abd al-Aziz Al Saud (1906-1975)

King Khaled bin Abd al-Aziz Al Saud (1913-1982)

King Abdullah bin Abd al-Aziz Al Saud (1923-2015)

Prince Muhammad bin Fahd Al Saud (1950)

Prince Khaled bin Faisal Al Saud (1941)

Prince Saud bin Faisal Al Saud (1941)

Prince Mitaib bin Abdullah Al Saud (1952)

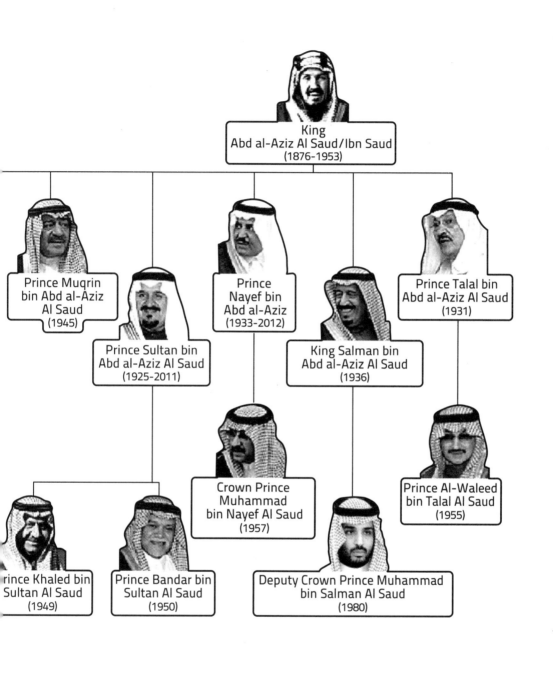

INTRODUCTION

REVOLUTION IN THE CAPITAL OF OIL?

For many years Saudi Arabia was thought of in the West primarily as a nation of oil sheikhs so wealthy that even their bathroom taps were made of gold. Funded by the revenues from the black gold, they might have come straight out of the *Adventures of Tintin*. They were depicted as organising orgies on the French Riviera and buying up half the stock of Harrods at the tail end of an afternoon, or else as riding their camels across the endless reaches of the desert in quest of new oil wells. Their wives were thought to be pathetic creatures, hidden at home and dressed in black from head to toe when in public. The holy places of Islam, moreover, were all in Saudi Arabia.

Yet in the aftermath of the 9/11 attacks the sheikhs had all suddenly turned into Sunni extremists, led by Osama bin Laden and plotting to blow up the world. Radical clerics preached hatred of anyone who disagreed with them, whether Muslim or infidel, inciting the hordes of Saudi youth to sow terror in the name of al-Qaeda abroad and eventually in their own country too.

Today, however, the Saudi youth seem largely to have turned their backs on extremism. Now we wonder whether they will remain immune to the influence of all the other young Arabs who have revolted, with varying degrees of success, against authoritarian regimes during the past few years. After all, Saudi Arabia, although it is a wealthy oil-producing country, has many of the same problems as Egypt, Tunisia and Syria, including an

1

extremely young population, high youth unemployment, repression and corruption.

This has proved an extremely explosive mix in other Arab countries, so it would not be entirely surprising if huge demonstrations were suddenly to occur on the streets of Riyadh or Jeddah, leading to the downfall of the royal house, with the princes going into exile in the United States and a revolutionary regime seizing power. Oil would of course continue to be tapped, because the new rulers would also need money to finance their new order, but the whole Gulf region could follow suit with emirs falling in swift succession and the revenues that once kept the established conservative order in power now filling the coffers of revolutionary movements in Jordan, Morocco, Egypt and Yemen. Israel would be boxed into a corner, and the West lost for a response.

Day of Rage

Yet so far nothing of that kind has happened in Saudi Arabia, although it is true that the years of protests by the Shiite minority in the eastern part of the country about their status as second-class citizens are a running sore. The Saudi authorities are certainly uneasy about them, particularly in view of their powerful Shiite neighbour, Iran, whom they suspect of stirring up trouble. So far, however, there is no indication that Shiite demonstrations have got out of hand, let alone that they have had any knock-on effect on the Sunni majority.

When an appeal for a Saudi 'Day of Rage' was launched on Facebook in the spring of 2011, the year of Arab insurgencies, it was almost immediately shared by tens of thousands of other Facebook users. But on the actual Day of Rage, 11 March, only a single demonstrator, Khaled al-Johani, defied the impressive police presence in the capital Riyadh. A number of measures, including intimidation (the police presence), bribery (King Abdullah had made an initial promise of 36 billion dollars for jobs, pensions and other social benefits and housing, with much more to come later) and religious sanctions (the grand mufti had forbidden demonstrations as being un-Islamic) had done their work and everyone stayed at home. Al-Johani was arrested and only released eighteen months later.

INTRODUCTION

Two years after the Day of Rage, a group of women psychology students at the Princess Nora University in Riyadh cite the results of social and political upheaval in Egypt and Syria with dismay. To be sure, the situation is not perfect in the kingdom, the young women argue. But while there is plenty of unemployment, the last few years have seen changes for the better and any comparison with the situation in Egypt is misleading. They conclude that an uprising is 'not the best way' to bring about improvements. On the contrary, they fear war in the streets, as in Syria. And Egypt too is in chaos. 'There are other options.'

Of course, these are the views of privileged young middle-class women. Their parents may not be extremely wealthy, but they are still rich enough to provide their children with a first-class education and they are comfortable with their daughters aspiring to a career and wanting to continue their studies abroad. Support of this kind is essential in Saudi Arabia, because without the backing of her guardian (father or brother), it is impossible for a woman to gain an education or pursue a career. While it may be true that all sorts of things are changing for the better in the kingdom, the formal position of a woman is still that of a minor.

When we visited the kingdom in 2013 these students also praised the role of the king—'It isn't difficult to tell our king if something is wrong; he listens to you.' Abdullah had the reputation of being a reformer, albeit a cautious one. Approval of the king appeared almost unanimous and, in the absence of any calls for revolt, this popularity was unquestionably an important factor. But these positive feelings did not extend to the bureaucratic strata beneath him, and there is genuine frustration about unemployment, poor housing and corruption among the less privileged.

At the moment Saudi Arabia is peaceful, but whether it will remain so is doubtful. On 16 March 2013 a popular religious leader, Salman al-Awda, posted an open letter on Facebook and Twitter to warn that the government urgently needs to listen to the complaints of its citizens if the country is to avoid a conflagration. Whether his fears are valid, or whether the combined forces of extreme puritanism, the monarchy and the revenues from oil will be capable of putting out any revolutionary fire, is an open question. The aim of this book is to consider all sides of this question by looking at a number of potential scenarios, ranging from that of business-as-usual to a complete break with the existing order.

DO NOT FEAR YOUR ENEMIES

THE CLERGY AND THE ROYAL FAMILY: UNITY IS STRENGTH

From time to time the Saudi authorities launch a half-hearted campaign to attract foreign tourists to the country. In 2000 a national tourism committee was instituted, but the promised tourist visas never actually materialised and it remains virtually impossible to enter the country except as a Muslim pilgrim or with a business visa. Every year pilgrims come in the millions, but their main goal is the holy places to which no non-Muslim tourist is even permitted entry.

It is not that there is nothing in Saudi Arabia for foreign tourists to enjoy. In the north-west there is Mada'in Saleh for instance, with its 131 tombs dating from the first century AD, predating Islam and the House of Saud. In 2008, UNESCO, the cultural organisation of the United Nations, placed the region on the World Heritage List, the first Saudi monument to receive this recognition. It is no coincidence that the tombs resemble the pink tombs hacked out of the rock in Petra in Jordan which have been visited by millions of tourists, as Petra was the capital of the kingdom of the Nabateans (586 BC–AD 600), and Mada'in Saleh was their second city.

A visit to Mada'in Saleh gives one a glimpse of a part of the history of the peninsula that is still comparatively unknown. It is a miracle that the tombs still exist, as Saudi Arabia has hardly any museums and anything that resembles art is still not tolerated by the generally exceptionally conservative clergy. The first impulse of the dominant, ultra-puritanical Wahhabi sect of Islam has been to destroy images and portraits on the grounds that they encourage idolatry. Tombs and other antiquities are also vulnerable to their iconoclastic onslaughts, as a result of which a great deal of the country's cultural and architectural heritage has been lost. In 2002, much to the fury of the Turkish government, the 220-year-old fort of the Ottoman Empire (1299–1923), Ajyad in Mecca, was mercilessly razed to the ground to make way for a gigantic hotel featuring a 601-metre high clock tower with the largest clock face in the world.

Nonetheless, changes have recently been taking place, and in 1999 a splendid, desert-coloured National Museum was opened in the capital Riyadh, which tells the story of both the cultural and political history of the pre-Islamic kingdoms in the peninsula, and the rise of the present Saudi royal dynasty. However, in the absence of any serious tourist industry there are few visitors, apart from noisy classes of school children, some expats and the occasional Saudi couple, perhaps eager to escape from prying eyes in the air-conditioned chill.

To gain an understanding of how Saudi society operates, one needs to hark back to Muhammad ibn (son of) Saud (c.1701–65), who waged a successful struggle against the ruling family of al-Dir'iyyah. Al-Dir'iyyah, or what remains of it, is a town just to the north-west of the present capital Riyadh, in the Nejd, the central region of the Arabian Peninsula. Due in part to the support of the deeply puritanical cleric, Muhammad ibn Abd al-Wahhab (1703–92), Ibn Saud became ruler of the first Saudi state.

Ibn Abd al-Wahhab was a Salafi reformer—reformer in the sense of purifier. He saw it as his mission to purify the faith as it was then practised of all impurities and superstitions. But his reforms proved more purge than purification. He ordered the demolition of tombs and holy places because the cult of the saints associated with them had become idolatrous. Smoking and music could only lead away from the one true God and were thus forbidden. The fact that in Saudi Arabia art and everything that smacks of idolatry is viewed to this day by the ulama (religious scholar) as haram (forbidden) is his achievement. He interpreted the Quran literally and the faithful were expected to conform as closely as possible to the precepts of that time.

Not everyone supported his drastic measures to restore an ancient and ideal Islam, and in 1744 he was banished from his birthplace of Uyayna,

30 kilometres from al-Dir'iyyah, after he had ordered a woman to be stoned to death for adultery. However, Muhammad ibn Saud made him welcome within his territories, concluding an agreement that they would combine forces to promote the true version of Islam.

The social anthropologist Madawi al-Rasheed quotes from their pact: 'This oasis is yours,' said Muhammad ibn Saud. 'Do not fear your enemies. By the name of God, if all Nejd was summoned to throw you out, we will never agree to expel you.'[1] 'You are the settlement's chief and a wise man,' Ibn Abd al-Wahhab answered. 'I want you to grant me an oath that you will perform *jihad* (holy war) against the unbelievers. In return you will be imam, leader of the Muslim community and I will be leader in religious matters.'[2]

This agreement still holds, its force undiminished, and the Wahhabi ulama, which is led to this day by a descendant of Ibn Abd al-Wahhab, continues to support the regime of the Al Saud. The latter does not interfere with religious matters. United, they reinforce each other.

In the National Museum the information available about the first Saudi state tells us there was chaos before the age of Ibn Abd al-Wahhab. Society had degenerated to such a degree that people worshiped stones and trees. Muhammad ibn Saud and Ibn Abd al-Wahhab instituted the laws of Islam to put a stop to this decadence; chaos was rooted out and peace restored. None of this, however, was enough to prevent the conquest of the state by the Ottoman Empire, and in 1818 al-Dir'iyyah capitulated after a bloody siege that lasted a year.

Masmak Fort

The fort of Masmak was built in the ancient centre of Riyadh close to the huge square where those who have been sentenced to death are decapitated. *Masmak* is an Arabic word meaning 'reinforce'. Like the National Museum, it is hardly a serious tourist attraction. Built of mud blocks, the edifice is neither large nor imposing, but nonetheless it was the scene of the first steps taken toward the unification of Saudi Arabia under the Saudi dynasty.

The fort was built around 1865. In 1902 the young Abd al-Aziz bin Abd al-Rahman Al Saud (1876–1953, better known as Ibn Saud) laid siege to it with a force of fifty men, taking it from the rival family of the Rashids, who themselves had taken it from the Sauds a couple of years previously. A fascinating film narrating these events can be viewed in the National Museum. Ibn Saud and his tiny army spent most of the night in prayer before stealing into the city at dawn to attack the fort. Confronted by the superior force of the defenders, Ibn Saud, brandishing his mighty sword, gained access to the building and slew the governor. After the fall of the fort, the citizens swore fealty to Ibn Saud, and Riyadh became the headquarters from which he founded the present state of Saudi Arabia. If we are to believe the film, this was both his dream and his destiny.

Yet a long series of wars had to be fought before the modern Kingdom of Saudi Arabia was finally created in 1932. The Rashids enlisted the help of the Ottoman Empire and inflicted a defeat on Ibn Saud, who responded by founding the Ikhwan (Brothers) in 1912, a ferocious Bedouin militia that imposed the purification of Islam by force of arms. In the spirit of Ibn Abd al-Wahhab, anyone who did not share their faith had to choose between conversion or death. The Arabian Peninsula was also a battlefield during the First World War, with the Turks on one side and the British on the other. This was the scene of Lawrence of Arabia's campaigns: besides Ibn Saud, the British also backed Sharif Hussein bin Ali (1854–1931), the emir of the Hejaz who proclaimed the Arab Revolt against the Ottoman Empire in 1916. Ibn Saud and his Ikhwan finally defeated and expelled Sharif Hussein in 1925.

But success went to the heads of the Ikhwan. They turned their backs on all forms of modernisation, such as automobiles and the telegraph system, and Ibn Saud was unable to hold them in check. Had Ibn Abd al-Wahhab not commanded that all non-Wahhabis should be converted or slain? They carried out raids on Kuwait, Iraq and Transjordan, all of which were under British protection. In 1929 the Ikhwan's camel cavalry was slaughtered in the battle of Sabila by the machine guns of Ibn Saud, who could not afford to get involved in any open conflict with the British.

The discovery of oil in the united Kingdom of Saudi Arabia, the largest oil find in the world, changed everything. The warlord Ibn Saud became an international personality overnight, someone who was definitely worth knowing. In 1945 he met President Roosevelt on board a US warship in the Suez Canal and he later held discussions with Winston Churchill in the

Fayoum Oasis south of Cairo. The founder of Saudi Arabia died of a heart attack in 1953.

Since then Saudi Arabia has modernised outwardly. At the same time, the Quran remains the constitution, while the country is still governed on the basis of sharia. As tends to happen, the rougher edges of Wahhabi doctrine were smoothed over here and there. A middle class emerged that sent their children to foreign universities and discovered films and fashion shows. The royal family itself proliferated and the hordes of princes and princesses found they had a greater income from oil than they knew what to do with. It was impossible to spend it all on mosques and *zakat* (charity).

The Occupation of the Grand Mosque

In 1979 the Islamic revolution took place in Iran, the Shiite rival of Saudi Arabia; Soviet troops invaded another Islamic country, Afghanistan; and a group of fanatics occupied the Grand Mosque at the heart of the Islamic world in the Saudi holy city of Mecca. It was a pivotal year for Saudi society, changing the kingdom beyond recognition. The world in turn now had to deal with an ever more assertive Iran and with the emergence of al-Qaeda and other Muslim extremist groupings.

The Iranian revolution and the war in Afghanistan have received plenty of attention, but the occupation of the Grand Mosque is little known. In his book *The Siege of Mecca* (2007), Yaroslav Trofimov, foreign correspondent for *The Wall Street Journal* from 1999 to 2007, tells the story of the assault, the utterly incompetent response of the Saudi princes and the far-reaching consequences of these events for Saudi Arabia and the world. Trofimov spoke to witnesses, surviving occupiers and former supporters of the activists, but the Saudi authorities themselves have done their utmost to prevent the facts about this bloody episode coming to light.

Juhayman al-Utaibi (1936–80) was a grandson of a family of Ikhwan activists and he shared their puritanical faith. He was critical of the royal family, many of whom according to him had defected dangerously from the true doctrine. In this he could reckon on support from the most powerful elements of the ulama, eager to embrace such an uncompromising stance. With a group of 250 armed fanatics, on the day of the Islamic new century, 20 November 1979, he launched an attack on the mosque that houses the sacred Ka'aba, the black cube in the centre of the mosque. The degeneracy of the country and of the royal family, a family that made improper international alliances with Christian powers, allowed women to enter employment and tolerated football and other sinful activities, were signs in his view of the advent of the Mahdi, the Muslim Messiah.

Juhayman had found his Messiah in the form of a friend, a young man named Muhammad al-Qahtani (1935–80). Nobody had any forewarning of Juhayman's plans, so the group was able to enter the mosque without any difficulty as though they were just pilgrims. Once there, they proclaimed the advent of the Mahdi who would purge the world of all error.

The princes who commanded the army and the elite corps who were to deal with this insurgency initially dispatched their forces to the grounds of the mosque without an adequate strategy. They were slaughtered by their opponents, who were heavily armed fanatics and who had the advantage of cover in the terrain. Finally, the ulama reluctantly gave permission to use force to drive out the insurgents. After two weeks they succeeded in relieving the mosque, with the help of a French police commando unit that trained and instructed the Saudi troops from a distance, since infidels were not permitted to enter the holy city of Mecca. The official number of deaths was about 270, whereas the non-official estimate came to around 1,000. Most of the insurgents were captured and executed, including Juhayman. The supposed Mahdi had already been killed in battle—proof, were it needed, that he could not have been the real Mahdi.

The Islamic legitimacy of the Saudi royal family had already received a blow from the claim of the revolutionary leadership in Iran to represent the one true Islam, and Juhayman's revolt further undermined its position. Its response was to send hosts of volunteers and almost unlimited funds to the Afghan jihad against the Soviet occupiers, and they also undertook a far-reaching Islamic revival in their own country, especially in education. This new educational system, which instilled intolerance in young minds, was a seedbed for all the extremists who emerged in the early 1990s, and who turned against the royal family itself after 2003.

If you talk to members of the Saudi middle classes, they will tell you how the country changed in the 1980s and 1990s. The journalist Samar Fatany, from Jeddah, is the daughter of a diplomat and has studied abroad:

We all returned and wanted to help our country become prosperous and modern. The idea was that women should get a chance to work, but our optimism didn't last long. While it didn't change all that abruptly, you genuinely felt that things were getting difficult by the mid-1980s. The 1990s were the worst, with most of the foreign community leaving and fashion shows and every form of entertainment being banned as sinful; this sort of freedom no longer existed.

No opera has ever been staged in the opera house in Riyadh, built just before 1979. Films were also prohibited. This was the epoch when screens were erected for the first time in restaurants between the male customers and family groups. The mutawwa, or 'Committee for the Promotion of Virtue and Prohibition of Vice', inspected construction plans to ensure that they complied with the moral principles of Islam.

The violent extremism, which was a by-product of the re-Islamisation of the 1980s and 1990s, was first put to the test, however, not in Saudi Arabia but in Afghanistan. The jihad against the Soviet occupation was backed by both the ulama and the population, which dispatched thousands of its sons to the war-torn country. The historian Dr Hatoon Ajwad al-Fassi clearly recalls the times:

We had the feeling that something was happening in the world of Islam and that it was our duty to help other people in their hour of need. It was dramatic and romantic. I saw the revival of Islam, not as a weapon in a struggle but as a way that Islam could once more play a role as a leader of civilisation. I had overlooked the fact that others had mobilised in order to militarise Islam and to interpret it in the most extreme way possible.

Osama bin Laden was one of the young Saudis who set off post-haste for Afghanistan. First of all they lent support to the mujahedeen, the Afghan-Muslim warriors, and later, after the Soviet withdrawal in 1989, it was the turn of the non-Wahhabi, but equally puritanical, Taliban. Saudi money was sent to radical mosques in various parts of the world and to the madrassas (Islamic schools) in Pakistan.

Increased radicalisation

The arrival of hundreds of thousands of American soldiers to the land of the holy cities of Mecca and Medina, in response to the Iraqi occupation of Kuwait in 1990, led to an even more intense radicalisation. The Grand Mufti, Sheikh Abd al-Aziz bin Baz (1910–99), justified the presence of the Americans on the grounds that this was an extreme situation. Many other clerics, however, openly condemned his fatwa. In mosques and schools the faithful were incited to act against the infidels.

Fifteen of the nineteen hijackers involved in Osama bin Laden's 2001 attack on the United States were Saudis. This was the logical result of all the support for the jihad against the infidel in Afghanistan, of its justification by the ulama and the subversion of the youth in the 1990s. The response of the royal family was to turn a blind eye, initially at least, and do nothing to restore things to their default, pre-9/11 situation.

In the second half of the 1990s, Bin Laden added the Saudi royal family to his list of mortal enemies. In furious pronouncements he castigated them for allowing American troops to be quartered on Arabian soil. These included his 1996 'Declaration of War Against the Americans Occupying the Land of Two Holy Places', in which he provided a detailed list of the crimes of the 'hypocritical' Saudi regime. According to the Quran, hypocrites 'will burn in the deepest pits of hell fire'.

After 11 September 2001, critical questions were asked about the influence of the intolerant Wahhabi sect and of the role of the ulama in Saudi education. Despite the fact that some Saudi ulama openly supported Bin Laden in their sermons, the royal family seemed unperturbed. Extremist clerics could continue to make death threats to internal, secular enemies and external Israeli and American foes, provided they did not explicitly threaten their own regime.

Things only changed after 12 May 2003, when thirty-five people were slaughtered in a series of synchronised suicide attacks on three residential estates for foreigners in Riyadh. The most radical clerics were arrested—the regime finally acknowledged the danger in their midst and changed course accordingly.

The security forces were merciless in their pursuit of Muslim extremists, the media became more open and it was again possible to question the way in which some religious leaders interpreted the faith. The principle that required Muslims to be hostile towards all other faiths was removed from school textbooks.

Yet these changes were anything but universally accepted. Take the case of Muhammad al-Harbi, a teacher in the city of al-Bakiria. In 2005 he was condemned to three years in prison and 750 lashes, at a rate of fifty a week. According to the Saudi press, al-Harbi had used newspaper articles to warn his pupils against the dangers of extremism and terrorism. The judge argued that he had mocked Islam, that he had undermined the faith of the students and encouraged heresies.

A few years later, Dr Khalil al-Khalil, a security specialist and at the time a member of the Majlis al-Shura, the consultative council appointed by the king, declared that a great deal had changed for the better, although, unlike many other informed Saudis, he still saw extremism as 'very dangerous'. 'It is not over. Don't underestimate the extremists,' he said. 'They are not lunatics, but well-organised groups. They have international contacts and are well trained.'

What had improved in his view was the fact that the population had become sensitised to the threat the extremists posed. But education still remained problematic. 'The extremists controlled education almost entirely and while we are now alert to the danger of this, how do we get rid of all of them? This cancer is a human problem—it's the teachers, not the books.'

Shopping malls

A visitor to Riyadh or Jeddah will be confronted by extremely modern edifices rising next to even more daring, avant-garde buildings under construction. The most expensive clothes by international couturiers and the scantiest lingerie are on display in gleaming shopping malls. Next to Ikea is McDonald's. You would think that a decisive shift had taken place towards secular or 'infidel' values. Ibn Abd al-Wahhab, the Ikhwan and Osama bin Laden would seem to have bitten the dust.

But don't be fooled, says the British historian and biographer Robert Lacey, author of the bestsellers *The Kingdom* (1981) and *Inside the Kingdom* (2009). He believes Wahhabi Islam is alive and well, and that the opposition against the king comes largely from conservative quarters:

Clerics protest against greater rights for women and the discussions on Twitter show clearly that the majority of Saudis are conservative. That's the problem in Saudi

Arabia, not the relatively isolated pro-democracy activists like my friend Muhammad al-Qahtani [a liberal human rights activist, sentenced to ten years in prison in March 2013]. The basis of the opposition is formed by deeply unhappy clerics who think that the government is too tolerant towards people like Al-Qahtani with their western ideas. Conservative Saudis, including women, believe that if you give women a voice in the Shura, you'll wake up next morning with a host of unmarried mothers.

Lacey, who has lived in Saudi Arabia for four years, says that there is an undercurrent of discontent and that no one is entirely satisfied with what they have:

The traders in Jeddah are angry about the preferential treatment given to businessmen in Nejd, the south thinks the north gets too much and there are so many different sorts of factions. The House of Saud is caught in the middle and tries to preserve a balance between all these different demands in what was formerly an extremely violent society.

The reason why many Saudis initially welcomed the Arab Spring was because they saw it was possible to achieve the dream of an Islamic regime through democratic means. For the Saudi monarchy, on the other hand, the Arab uprisings posed a new danger.

Many young Saudis, however, will now tell you that democracy is rapidly losing its appeal after everything that has gone wrong in Egypt and Syria.

2

THE TWO-EDGED SWORD OF ISLAM

THE HOLY ALLIANCE UNDER FIRE

The eighteenth-century mutual aid pact between Ibn Saud and Ibn Abd al-Wahhab holds good to this day. Under the terms of this ancient alliance, which might also be described as a power-sharing arrangement, the Wahhabi clerics, or at least the established ulama, guarantee the political legitimacy of the House of Saud. In its turn the royal family continues to refrain from any basic interference with the ultra-puritanical Sunni foundations of the country insisted on by the conservative clergy. All dangers have thus been averted up until now, but there are new threats on the horizon.

It has not always gone that smoothly in the past, and both parties have had to make concessions. In 1960 Crown Prince Faisal bin Abd al-Aziz Al Saud (1906–75) introduced education for girls. But he was only able to do that on Islamic terms, with the argument that literate women would later make better wives and mothers. He pushed TV broadcasting through in 1963 in exchange for promises that it would be kept within the bounds of decency and that there would be no shortage of religious programmes. And it was TV, incidentally, which was to lead to his assassination. A fanatical distant cousin of his was shot dead during an attack on the new TV building and a brother of the cousin avenged his death in 1975.

During the occupation of the Grand Mosque in Mecca in 1979, which was a protest against the moral decline of the royal family, the princes had to

15

go to great lengths to get the ulama to give their blessing to an attack on the fanatical occupiers. Without this approval they would never have dared resort to the violent action required to recover the sacred building and its grounds. In return the royal family had to tolerate a lengthy period of radical Islamisation to redress the balance. This led to morbid excesses among the preachers of the Sahwa movement (*sahwa* means 'awakening') who paved the way for international Islamic terrorist attacks with their hate sermons against Jews, Christians and any Muslims who had a different viewpoint on Islam from themselves. Later, when the terror turned against the princes, the royal family resorted to drastic measures to rectify the situation. But in the end the clergy has always helped the royal family to survive.

Rubber stamp

With the arrival of the twenty-first century, neither the royal family nor the clerics can continue to isolate the country from the rest of the world; the Internet and satellite TV have made all borders obsolete. The Arab world is in turmoil and even the Saudis are affected by notions of revolt. Once again, however, in 2011, it was the ulama that got the royal family out of a sticky situation, when appeals started being posted on Facebook after the example of Tunisia and Egypt, calling for people to go on to the streets and demonstrate. The Grand Mufti, Abd al-Aziz Al al-Sheikh, denounced all demonstrations as non-Islamic, because they did nothing but spread chaos. 'Protests such as these have no relation whatsoever to Islam, because Islam prefers dialogue,' he said.[1] Only one demonstrator showed up.

It is questionable how independent the clergy still is when it continues to give government policies its seal of approval. Has it become a rubber stamp of religious correctness for measures that the royal family for one reason or another deems necessary, legitimising them in the eyes of the more conservative strata of society? In forbidding demonstrations for instance, or years previously, in 1990, when it turned a blind eye to the presence of infidel American troops in the Land of the Two Holy Mosques? What is clear is that the clergy itself is divided between an 'establishment' on the one hand and less predictable religious leaders on the other. It was not without cause that in 2010 King Abdullah decreed that only the highest ulama had the authority to issue fatwas. However, the non-established clerics have the Internet instead of fatwas.

Even though he was perhaps a little more cautious than his half-brother Faisal, Abdullah was also a reformer. The clergy object to Abdullah's reforms today with the same fury as they previously protested against Faisal's introduction of education for girls. Now, however, they make their views known on Twitter, Facebook or other social media. The fact that they want to prevent these social reforms being implemented does not mean that they eschew modern means of communication. On the contrary, there are clerics who can boast millions of followers on Twitter, even if critics insinuate that a fair proportion of them have been bought.

In February 2013, thirty educated women, veiled and clad in black from top to toe, were installed as members of the Consultative Council, the Majlis al-Shura. In so doing, King Abdullah fulfilled a promise he had made two years earlier. Women were also granted suffrage for the next municipal elections. No other elections have as yet been announced.

It was an important reform. When the women were sworn in, the king summoned the grand mufti to attend the Majlis al-Shura to show TV viewers that his decision had received the blessing of the clerics, or at least of their establishment. The response of the radical ulama was immediate, savage and grotesquely rude. Ahmed Abd al-Qader, for instance, tweeted, 'They think they can mock at the mufti by giving these prostitutes a lawful position of power.' Another of them, Nasser al-Omar, warned against this 'Westernisation'—by which he meant everything that did not pass the test of Wahhabi doctrine. 'A corrupt beginning leads to corrupt results,' he tweeted.[2]

Some of the clerics were so furious that they demonstrated in person outside the court, perhaps forgetting the grand mufti's denunciation of street protests. In a YouTube video mentioned by the blogger Ahmed al-Omran of the informal press bureau, Riyadh Bureau, one of them says that 'these recent appointments in Shoura do not represent the good people'.[3]

Complaints

The appointment of female members to the Consultative Council was by no means the demonstrators' only objection. Al-Omran's Riyadh Bureau gave a summary of their grievances, which are a mixture of cultural and economic, radical and conservative issues. They were against book markets, literary clubs and cafés, and against greater freedom of expression in the media—developments which 'lead to ideological chaos and cultural dissoluteness'. They protested against the educational reforms that undermine the segregation of the sexes and the millions of euros spent on scholarships enabling large numbers of young Saudis to study abroad. This is one of the late king's most successful programmes and one that allows young people to become acquainted with other cultures.

The protesting clerics also lodged complaints against the 'normalising of gender mixing in society' by encouraging women to go and work in shops, industry, restaurants and the like.[4] This recent development in fact represents an enormous change in Saudi Arabia. An active job opportunity programme for women has been launched with the support of the king, without which of course it could not have happened. They also protested against the participation of two young women in the London Olympics in the summer of 2012—a grievance that was shared by the grand mufti, who declared, 'Women should be housewives. It isn't necessary for them to take part in sports'[5]—and opposed what they saw as the improper use of public funds, the absence of good housing, poor health services and the illegal detention of citizens.

Admittedly, these latter issues, which are very widely complained about, have nothing to do with Wahhabi Islam as such. The matters that often draw the attention of the Western media are the protests against sports activities for women and working women as being in conflict with the Islamic identity of the country. And sometimes it is indeed aged preachers from remote corners of the kingdom that get into the American and European news with their advice that baby girls should be required to wear veils so as not to provoke the lustful attentions of males.[6] Saudis themselves tend just to shrug their shoulders.

Not all radical Wahhabi clerics are unworldly mavericks. Take Sheikh Muhammad al-Arefe (b.1970), also one of those who is easily provoked, especially when it comes to diluting the segregation of men and woman (*ikhtilat*, the intermingling of the sexes). Al-Arefe, professor at the King Saud University in Riyadh, is high on the list of the most popular Saudi tweeters with 10.3 million followers at the time of writing. He is said to have bought some of his followers, and obviously not all of them are supporters, but nonetheless he does receive a huge amount of attention.

An example of a question to Muhammad al-Arefe on Twitter: What is the wise viewpoint on *ikhtilat*? And what is its proof? @MohamadAlarefe: '*Ikhtilat* is not permitted because it results in great evil. He has said: if you ask women something, you should do it behind a screen; that is better for you and for them.'

As Eman al-Nafjan writes in her blog 'Saudiwoman', al-Arefe is 'the complete package. He is the Brad Pitt of Sheikhdom.'[7] In other words, he is charismatic: 'it almost seems like he has hypnotic super-powers,' she goes on. 'Even women will accept being told that they are less than men when it comes from his mouth.' Yet there are YouTube films in which he advises men not to hit their wives too hard. They should not hit them so hard that they 'make their faces ugly', but beat them, they may.

It goes without saying that al-Arefe is also against women driving cars and he is supported in this by the grand mufti, because 'women driving would lead to more accidents. When women are in danger, they don't know how to behave. How would they deal with accidents?'[8] According to al-Arefe, the women in Riyadh who received harsh penalties for protesting against this restriction by driving through the streets in 1991 should never have been allowed to work again at the universities after their years of suspension. After all, these were liberal women, and now they can spread their ideas again. Al-Nafjan says that al-Arefe has proposed that a law be drafted to prevent liberal women from promoting their sinful ideas as teachers at schools or in universities. They would have to stick to the letter of the textbooks.

Al-Arefe's controversial statements were not limited to women. In a TV interview in February 2013, al-Arefe said that Osama bin Laden had been subjected to character assassination and that al-Qaeda did not tolerate blood being shed.[9] On the other hand he said on TV that 'the desire to shed blood, to break skulls and to hack off limbs in God's cause and in defence of their religion is undoubtedly honourable for the faithful'.[10]

During a conference in Cairo in June 2013 he called for a holy war in Syria, to be conducted 'in every possible fashion'. But this did not prevent him from proceeding to London, which he had earlier described, according to the Saudi satellite broadcaster al-Arabiya, as 'a place that Muslims should not visit in times of crisis'.[11] Al-Arefe tweeted from London to say that 'I've mixed with the British public in London and found them to be pleasant, polite & respectful towards all religions.'[12] The Saudi newspaper *Okaz* announced that he was recording his new TV programme there, *My Trip with al-Arefe*. Al-Arefe was banned from Britain in June 2014, accused of inciting young British men to fight in Syria or Iraq. He denies having said this.

Danger

Back home in Saudi Arabia he was placed under house arrest, as one can read on his Facebook page—the authorities, however, said nothing about this. According to a colleague of al-Arefe, his public support for the deposed Egyptian president, Mohamed Morsi, and his appeal to the authorities to support Morsi was the reason for this measure. The government supports the 2013 military coup against Morsi and his Muslim Brotherhood, as evidenced by the billions of dollars of aid given to post-coup Egypt.

Once again, it is clear that the clerics in Saudi Arabia have plenty of freedom to say what they like and that the authorities only take action when government interests are threatened. The jihad in Syria against the regime of Bashar al-Assad has the support of the monarchy; al-Arefe is entitled to applaud this holy war, whereas support for Morsi is strictly forbidden. After all, his Muslim Brotherhood is a revolutionary Islamic reform movement that has no sympathy for conservative monarchies and is therefore seen as dangerous.

But how dangerous is al-Arefe? It is true that he is said to have more than 10 million 'followers' but it is hard to take him seriously when you look at his YouTube clips. He is clearly someone who likes the glare of publicity. Maybe he is more controversial than radical—his cheerful trip to London, which he called 'a place that Muslims should not visit in times of crisis', suggests this. Is he not a Muslim, or is there no crisis?

The same cannot be said of Sheikh Salman al-Awda, who is also one of the most popular clerics on Twitter. In his radical youth this cleric spent many years in prison. Born in 1956, al-Awda was a powerful advocate of the jihad in Afghanistan against the Soviet occupation. The gist of his teaching was that the only authentic way of proselytising for Wahhabi Islam was by violence. In this he was no different from Muhammad Ibn Abd al-Wahhab, who also spread his beliefs through the sword.

In itself this was not the problem for the authorities. The reason he was sent to prison was his role in the Sahwa movement, which campaigned fiercely for strict adherence to the values of Islam, while denouncing corruption, secularisation, the liberalisation of society and even what it saw as the readiness of the higher ranks of the ulama to come to the aid of the monarchy. In 1990, for instance, al-Awda and other Sahwa clerics carried out a vigorous campaign against the presence of American and other foreign forces in the peninsula. The Grand Mufti Abd al-Aziz bin Baz, representing establishment opinion, had given his blessing to the influx of foreign troops; he should therefore be removed from his position, they claimed, along with the other members of the ulama establishment who only concerned themselves with theological niceties and not with the degeneration of society. The Sahwa and al-Awda took matters a step further, however, and conducted a campaign for far-reaching reform in both domestic and foreign policy. Among other things, they organised widely supported petitions calling for more general popular representation, a stricter application of sharia law, the breaking of relations with infidel governments and the creation of a separate army to wage war on Israel. All this was totally unacceptable to the monarchy. Al-Awda and hundreds of others were sent to prison in 1994. In 1999 he was set free, a changed man. He had become a moderate.

Eman al-Nafjan gave a telling example of this in her blog in 2008: 'My sister saw him in a mall in Dubai with his wife and kids. The real shocker is that his wife was wearing a niqab [veil] and her abaya [ankle-length robe] was on her shoulders and NOT tent style over her head! That's the Saudi equivalent of seeing a priest's wife sunbathing topless.'[13]

In the 1990s al-Awda was viewed as a supporter of Bin Laden, but in 2007 he published a sensational open letter addressed to 'my brother Osama' in which he turned his back on the al-Qaeda leader. He held him responsible for the American occupation of Muslim soil in Afghanistan and Iraq:

Brother Osama, how much blood has been spilled? How many innocent children, women and old people have been killed, maimed, and expelled from their homes in the name of 'al-Qaeda'? Are you happy to meet Allah with this heavy burden on your shoulders? It is a weighty burden indeed—at least hundreds of thousands of innocent people, if not millions.[14]

In 2009 he sent a similar letter to Bin Laden's second man (and leader of al-Qaeda after 2011), Ayman al-Zawahiri. In it he reminded the Egyptian that he is no cleric—al-Zawahiri was originally a paediatrician—and that he wanted to know who had given him permission to make pronouncements about serious religious matters such as *takfir* (declaring someone an infidel) and aggression.

Sheikh al-Awda is currently seen as a mainstay of the monarchy, who receives protection from the court in return. Has he really been tamed, however? There are plenty of signs that he is increasingly presenting himself as a champion of reforms and a potential leader of the opposition. It seems as though it is not the radical but vain al-Arefe who represents the greatest danger for a conservative monarchy, but a penitent like Salman al-Awda. In a remarkable development he wrote a book, *Questions of Revolution* (2012), in which he endorsed peaceful revolution, in direct conflict with the concepts of the establishment clergy. He published it on the Internet after it was banned.

It is worth taking another look at the open letter he posted in March 2013 on Facebook and Twitter. It is a severe warning to the regime—if you do not carry out reforms, the country will burn. He is speaking honestly and as a friend, he begins. 'We must preserve the gains we have made. ... The alternative is chaos, disintegration and strife.'[15] Al-Awda, like so many Saudis, especially among the young, is looking at the results of the popular uprisings in Egypt, Libya and Syria and does not want anything to do with them.

However, he warns, 'people here are the same as they are everywhere else in the world. They have their ambitions, their demands and their rights. They will not remain silent forever if some or all of these things are constantly denied to them. Negative feelings have been accumulating for a long time. I draw what I am saying from numerous people hailing from all sectors and regions of our society. ... When people cease being afraid, you can expect them to do anything, and if their anger gets to a critical point, then nothing will be able to placate them. When tempers are high, religious, political and cultural symbols lose their value. The mob in the streets takes control.'[16]

It will be like Syria, he means. He then goes on to discuss prisons and prisoners—he detects hatred, vengefulness, extremism and a violation of human rights, and this has led to protests by the wives of prisoners. Nobody should remain in detention except those whose crimes are proven and who have been sentenced for them. 'It is dangerous to restrict people to the point that they feel they have nothing more to lose. A citizen's rights are legitimate and inalienable. They are not a courtesy.'[17]

He sums up the causes of the tension in the country as follows: fiscal and administrative corruption, unemployment, poor housing, poverty, lack of a good health service and proper provisions for education and an absence of any genuine prospect of political reform. So he identifies exactly the same problems in Saudi Arabia, which is a wealthy oil-producing nation, as those that brought people out on to the streets to bring about the downfall of their authoritarian rulers in much poorer countries like Tunisia and Egypt. Things cannot go on like this for much longer, he writes. The question, however, remains of what path to follow.

Possibly mindful of his period in prison, al-Awda remains extremely cautious in his advice about what action to take. His suggestions come in the form of questions. 'How can a country that relies upon personal connections instead of institutions ever hope to face real challenges?' And: 'The people, especially our young people, are asking: Where are the channels of communication between us and our leaders?'[18] In other words, a form of popular representation is called for, something he also argued for in his Sahwa years.

No rational person wants to start a fire that will reduce his country to ashes, al-Awda says; nobody wants violence to be the method by which we express ourselves. 'The only solution is to take wise and timely decisions before violence is kindled.'[19] Is it possible to imagine Sheikh Salman al-Awda as a leader of the Saudi revolution? The regime is certainly not happy at the thought. At the end of July 2013 they banned his new TV show, *You Have Rights*. Cracks are beginning to appear in the time-hallowed alliance of mutual support between the ulama and the monarchy. It is potentially a very dangerous development.

3

OIL, OIL, GLORIOUS OIL

AN UNCERTAIN ROAD

Petrol is cheap in Saudi Arabia—dirt cheap. Fuel costs 16 dollar cents per litre. That is good news of course for Saudis who drive a car, which they almost all do because public transport is more or less non-existent. The country is a paradise for owners of petrol-guzzling SUVs. The drawback is that the domestic consumption of oil has consistently increased over the years and at a certain point there will be none left to export. Recent estimates indicate that this may well be the case in about fifteen years if there is no change in government policy.[1]

That would be a calamity, because 80 to 90 per cent of the state budget is based on revenues from oil.[2] The economy would grind to a halt. Not only that, but over the years there would be less and less money available for purchasing the loyalty of Saudi citizens through the system of subsidies, grants, job-creating schemes and scholarships. And that could easily be the signal for a 'Saudi Spring'. 'In the short term everything in the garden is lovely,' said a senior employee at Saudi Aramco, who prefers to remain anonymous.[3] He is giving us his picture of the future of his country:

Some experts argue that in a few years' time we will need the price of oil to remain at well above $100 a barrel of oil in order not to go into the red. In the past two years the price of a barrel has fluctuated around this sum, so that's very positive. But even if it dropped to 70 dollars, it won't lead to serious problems immediately, not even with higher government outlays that we have had since the start of 2011 in response to the Arab uprisings.

Ten years ago the 'break-even' price still averaged at around $20. Paul Sampson of the online news media group 'Energy Intelligence' is also not someone who panics easily:

How can anyone seriously describe Saudi Arabia's economic outlook as 'bleak'? The country is earning close to $300 billion per year in oil export revenues—a staggering amount of money—and has more than $600 billion in foreign currency reserves.[4] This does not suggest any impending crisis to me—rather it is a fantastic platform to build on. I can't understand why there are so many gloomy pieces about Saudi; it doesn't make any sense to me. Or am I missing something?[5]

Other economists strike a more pessimistic note. For instance, Robert Looney, the author of a number of standard works about oil and development in the Gulf states, reckoned that in 2015 Saudi Arabia needed a price of $90 a barrel.[6] Others, like the Institute for International Finance, give $110 as a base price, while the Deutsche Bank estimated that the 2015 budget break-even price will be somewhere in-between (i.e. $104.5).[7] As oil prices have declined substantially since mid-2014, while government spending has increased, Saudi Arabia is on course to run a budget deficit in 2015, the first since 2011 and the largest in its history.[8] Based on projections by Riyadh-based Jadwa Investment, Looney estimates that Saudi Arabia's break-even, inflation-adjusted oil price will increase to $175 in 2025 and even $320 by 2030.[9]

The impact of subsidies

Abdel Aziz Aluwaisheg regularly sounds the alarm about the ever-increasing domestic consumption of oil in the English-language Saudi daily *Arab News*. He sums up the bare facts as follows: 'The cost of this waste is staggering: At $100 a barrel, domestic consumption is depriving Saudi Arabia of nearly 150 billion of foreign earnings per year.'[10] John Sfakianakis, a seasoned expert on the Saudi economy, provides more detail:

On an annual basis, Saudi Arabia's consumption is twice that of the United States and around four times that of Germany, which has an economy five times the size of that of the kingdom. Energy use per head is also rising, and between 2000 and 2010, domestic oil consumption jumped by around 30 percent …[11] In 2013, a quarter of total Saudi oil production was consumed domestically.[12]

To a large extent this is obviously due to the ludicrously low price of petrol. According to Aluwaisheg:

There are about 10 million passenger cars in the country, the number growing by about 5 percent annually … Saudis' preference for gas guzzlers is fuelled by incredibly cheap gasoline prices. Because of cheap and abundant energy, Saudi Arabia has not developed mass transit systems. It relies mostly on private cars, not public transportation to move residents to their places of work, schools, shopping and entertainment.[13]

Less than 2 per cent of the population of Riyadh (6 million) makes any use of the public transport 'system', which consists of some rather ramshackle buses and minibuses. So long as petrol costs almost nothing, nothing will change. A price rise would seem the obvious solution, but would the government dare?

It would be going too far to say that a 'broad social debate' is being held on this subject; slowly but surely, however, the realisation is dawning among wider circles of society that things cannot go on like this. Even Muhammad al-Sabban, the government's principal oil advisor for many years, and someone not exactly known for his radical ideas, has sounded the alarm:

Rapid growth in consumption is a real problem that can't continue in any way. … The main problem with subsidies in Saudi Arabia is that they are becoming an economic burden on the government as they benefit all classes, including the rich and expats, and not only the low-income classes. Reviewing fuel prices in Saudi Arabia is inevitable, if not a priority.[14]

And sometimes something does happen. In the summer of 2013 the government announced its plans to build a 176-kilometre underground network in the capital. Foreign companies will build the six lines on which driverless electric trains will run. The total expenditure will amount to $22.5 billion, and the network is due to come into operation in 2019. Comparable plans had previously been presented for Mecca and Jeddah. For the relieved residents, it is high time:

'For sure I will use the metro—it will be a major solution for the women problem in our society, since we don't drive,' said Alaa Hassan, a female university student in Riyadh. 'I go to my university by minibus and I pay SR2,000 [$535] per month; other classmates who live nearer pay 800 to 1,000. For sure the metro will be cheaper.'[15]

It is not just the explosive increase in the number of car owners that is to blame for the rise in the consumption of oil. Greater electricity consumption plays an important part too; for instance, there are the ubiquitous air conditioners which it is not uncommon for Saudis to leave on while they are away on holiday.[16] The electricity tariff in Saudi Arabia is the lowest in the world. A substantial 20 per cent of the daily production of oil—around 9.5 million barrels per day—is required to generate energy.[17] Experts claim that if nothing changes, this figure will have doubled by around 2030, knowing that the Saudi population is estimated to increase to 45 million in 2050. Fatih Birol, chief economist for the International Energy Agency, also points at the wasteful manner in which oil is being used: 'To use oil for electricity is absolutely very uneconomic,' he says. 'It's like using Chanel perfume to fuel your car.'[18] Even the elite are beginning to get the message, with Prince Abd al-Aziz bin Salman Al Saud, the assistant minister for petroleum and mineral resources, calling for urgent action to reduce domestic energy consumption or 'risk harming Saudi export volumes in the future'.[19]

One way of dealing with this problem, the assistant minister advised, would be the gradual switching from oil to natural gas as a fuel for power stations. This is now beginning to happen. And there is even more good news, at least on paper. In 2010 the government floated a plan for a quarter of the production of electricity to be generated by wind and solar energy by 2032. 'Since that landmark unveiling in 2010, however, very few concrete actions have been taken in terms of deploying projects,' writes Vahid Fotuhi, president of the Emirates Solar Industry Association.[20] And while Oil Minister al-Naimi has optimistically argued that Saudi Arabia could export electricity produced from solar power instead of oil, most observers are more sceptical—though not completely negative. Eckart Woertz, for instance, argues that 'so far such high-flying plans are far from realisation … yet things are set to change'.[21] The plans for generating nuclear power would seem to be much more serious. Contracts have now been signed with France, South Korea, China and Argentina for the construction of sixteen reactors by 2030, which would then cover 20 per cent of its electricity needs.

The huge waste of water also plays a part in this excessive energy consumption. Saudi Arabia is one of the biggest users in the world (265 litres per person per day; in the Netherlands it is 121 litres; in the United States, however, each person uses about 340 litres of water per day). In itself that would not need to be a problem, if there were sufficient resources underground or in rivers and lakes or else from rainfall. This is hardly the case, however. While there are a few aquifers, or water-bearing substrata, these are rapidly being used up. Saudi Arabia consumes 936 per cent of its total renewable water resources every year.[22] Aluwaisheg of *Arab News* quotes a saying of the Prophet Muhammad that Muslims should above all be sparing in their use of water, 'even if they live on the shores of a river'. Clearly most Saudis ignore this advice. 'The favourite way of washing your car is with delicious tap water,' Aluwaisheg remarks drily. Because there is less and less water available, the country has to depend increasingly on desalination plants. These are not only extremely expensive, but are also bad for the environment and they guzzle energy. 'They account for 10 to 20 per cent of the entire consumption of energy in Saudi Arabia,' Aluwaisheg informs us. Water is expensive therefore, but the consumer is barely aware of this. Once again, subsidies are lavished on these plants and there is no stimulus whatsoever to use these systems sparingly.[23]

It is high time, Aluwaisheg and his fellow economists argue, to insist on a price that is related to the real situation, but what government would dare to do that?

Reducing subsidies would not only affect the average citizen in his pocket; it would also have an impact on the industrial sector which benefits from the low cost of raw materials and electricity. And then there are all those princes and princesses who never pay their electricity bills and get away with it. Nearly $720 million is owed by Saudi VIPs, with some arrears dating back nearly thirty years.[24] Who is doing anything about that?

Shale gas: optimists versus pessimists

'Shale Gas: The Energy Revolution'—in recent years this has been the head-line on the front page of many newspapers. The age of 'the new black gold' was predicted and shale gas (and shale oil) would be a 'game changer', lead-ing to a 'paradigmatic change', an era of 'abundance', and so on and so forth. According to Robin West, the CEO of the energy consultancy PCF Energy, the extraction of shale gas is nothing less than 'the energy equivalent of the fall of the Berlin Wall'.[25] Fracking would make it possible to extract huge reserves of oil and gas, the threat of energy shortages is no longer relevant and there is a whole new set of power relations on the oil market.

In the short term at least the optimists are being proven right. US pro-duction of crude oil, along with liquids separated from natural gas, sur-passed all other countries in 2014 with daily output exceeding 11 million barrels in the first quarter. The United States had already surpassed Russia in natural gas production in 2013, pulling ahead for the first time since 1982. In 2035 it will be entirely self-supporting.[26] 'Saudi America' was the provocative headline in *The Economist*.[27] The position of Saudi Arabia as the world's largest oil exporter will therefore not remain uncontested. In Riyadh, people would do well to be worried. 'In general, the coming of shale gas will magnify the importance of geography,' argued Robert Kaplan. 'Which countries have shale underground and which don't will help determine power relationships.'[28]

Diametrically opposed to the shale gas optimists is a group of more sceptical experts. They too deploy hyperboles to make their case—'the biggest oil swindle' and 'the myth of the coming of "Saudi America"'.[29] And this title of a book by Bill Powers is also self-explanatory: *Cold, Hungry and in the Dark: Exploding the Natural Gas Supply Myth* (2013). The web-site shalebubble.org welcomes its readers with the words: 'They tell us we're on the cusp of an oil & gas revolution. But what if it's all just a short-term bubble?' Maybe they do not need to worry in Riyadh after all.

It is hard to say who is right, given that the material is very complicated. Many experts argue that it is obvious that shale gas only has a bridging function en route to a new future for energy, free of fossil fuels. The same also goes for the most recent energy hype—that around methane hydrate or methane ice. Here too enormous supplies are supposed to be extractable in the near future, amounting to the next 'revolution'. Drill, baby, drill—that's the slogan. The largest supplies of this source of fuel ('ice that can burn') are located in Japan, China, India, North and South Korea, Taiwan, Norway, the United States and Canada.[30]

Does all this worry the Saudis? Ali al-Naimi, the minister of petroleum and mineral resources, does not see a problem—or so it seems. He never tires of repeating that everything in the garden is lovely. 'This is not the first time new sources of oil are discovered—don't forget history. There was oil from the North Sea and Brazil, so why is there so much talk about shale oil now?'[31] And he goes on to say reassuringly that 'There is enough demand growth to absorb new supplies and help maintain market stability.'[32] In May 2013 al-Naimi told a Washington audience that shale oil is 'great news' for the United States, and no threat to his own country.[33] In late 2014, however, after oil prices had been declining sharply, Saudi Arabia blocked calls from poorer members of the OPEC oil exporter group for production cuts to arrest this slide in global prices. It was speculated that al-Naimi had a price war in mind that might make some future US shale oil projects uncompetitive due to high production costs, thereby easing competitive pressures on OPEC in the longer term.

Well before oil prices started dropping, others in the kingdom had sounded the alarm bell. Take, for instance, Prince al-Waleed bin Talal Al Saud, not the least of the princes of the Saudi royal house. In late July 2013 he published a fourteen-page letter on Twitter, which he had sent to al-Naimi a couple of months before. The latter had apparently not bothered to reply and the prince must have felt that his best response was to put the letter in the public domain. Firmly but politely he wrote, 'We disagree with your excellency on what you said and we see that raising North American shale gas production is an inevitable threat.' The billionaire prince warned that there is a clear and increasing decline in demand for crude from members of the Organization of Petroleum Exporting Countries, particularly Saudi Arabia.[34]

Al-Waleed does not mention it, but the prospective competition from Saudi Arabia's neighbour Iraq is, if anything, an even greater threat, and Riyadh might also worry that Iranian—and possibly Libyan—oil production will swing upward again. For that matter, the Saudi oil supplies may also be smaller than the Saudi authorities have admitted. Two years ago it emerged via WikiLeaks that Sadad al-Husseini, the former executive vice president for exploration and production at Saudi Aramco, 'believes that Aramco's reserves are overstated by as much as 300 billion barrels of "speculative resources"'.[35] In other words, by 40 per cent. In the worst-case scenario therefore the oil reserves are less than is usually averred while at the same time the demand for Saudi oil is on the decline.

Economic cities

At least as important was al-Waleed bin Talal's remark about the country's continuing dependence on revenues from oil. He noted Saudi Arabia's reliance on oil to fund 92 per cent of the country's fiscal budget, which 'is contradicting many of the state's plans to diversify its income sources'.[36] In a more recent open letter, posted on Twitter on 13 October 2014, he added a warning against sliding oil prices, repeating his previous message that Saudi Arabia needed to reduce its reliance on crude oil and diversify its revenues. For years now the sorely needed diversification of the economy has been a matter for debate and for years the same conclusion has also been reached—that too little progress has been made. It is true that there has been some growth in the non-oil sector, but it has happened at a snail's pace. The processing industry amounts to only 10 per cent of the gross domestic production and 65 per cent of this is in the petrochemical industry. The non-oil sector's share of total investments has even declined in recent years.[37] The still very feeble private sector is in the hands of a small club of wealthy businessmen, who as a rule are linked to the government, which in turn is also dependent on revenues from oil.

Some people believe that the future lies in the 'economic cities' which King Abdullah has planned on the basis of a public–private partnership, ranging from high-tech to agriculture. They are expected to provide the necessary job opportunities for the indigenous population. The original idea was to build six of them, but this was later reduced to four. The best known is King Abdullah Economic City (KAEC), situated in Rabigh on the Red Sea. While the original cost was estimated at $86 billion, the project's website tells us that another 100 billion will be needed to complete the city.[38]

Whether everything will work out as planned is doubtful. In his book, *A Hologram for the King* (2012), Dave Eggers sketches a portrait of this megaproject that is as funny as it is shocking. One of his characters describes KAEC—which he pronounces as 'cake'—as 'a stillborn child'.[39] Another, somewhat more empathetic character calls it 'the dream of King Abdullah'.[40] Robert Lacey, who is generally critical but polite about Saudi Arabia, is thoroughly pessimistic. 'These economic cities are a farce,' he says in an interview.

The journalist Karen Elliot House agrees with Lacey. In her book *On Saudi Arabia* (2012) she draws a piquant comparison:

Government plans in Saudi Arabia are like those in the old Soviet Union, grandiose but unmet … Whenever one grand plan fails, government spinners all too often react by announcing a new one, under a newly designated government agency, with a new acronym, a new headquarters, and of course, a new budget.[41]

There are problems and uncertainties on many fronts then. The Saudi government cannot of course do much about uncertainties such as the 'dangers' implicit in the extraction of shale gas in North America.[42] This is all the more reason for it to face up to the problems, but that would require political will. Since the Arab Spring, this is even less likely than before. In 2011 the king opted for the line of least resistance by offering plenty of money and many other sweeteners to keep people happy. There was, and is, hardly any readiness to tackle the real issues. A hike in the price of petrol is just one possible step. The really tricky issue is imposing taxes, although this may become essential in the (near?) future. There is no such thing as income tax in Saudi Arabia. Suppose the government does impose it on its subjects, will they not want to have more of a say in matters?

'Little America'

Pay a visit to the Saudi Aramco Residential Camp in Dhahran, in the east of Saudi Arabia, and you might easily imagine you are in a California suburb. 'Little America' is the right nickname for this compound which houses the employees and family of the biggest oil firm in the world. There are low bungalows, green lawns and wide streets full of cars with women drivers. You have an appointment with one of the first feminists in the country, Wajeeha al-Huwaider, and she picks you up personally in her own car. All this takes place, of course, inside the fences of the compound, where she is free of the often deeply intrusive mutawwa, the religious police who are kept firmly outside.

'Little America', with its population of around 11,000, is like a fortress city, complete with its own schools, cinemas, swimming pools, golf courses, libraries and shops. Until the 1980s you were even permitted to consume alcohol, eat pork and celebrate Christmas in the compound. Since Islamisation set in after 1979 social customs are no longer so easy-going, but, unlike the rest of the country, Catholic, Protestant and Mormon religious services take place within the walls of three gymnasia. The Muslim religion is almost invisible and the minaret of the local mosque is quite small. Men and women mix in relaxed fashion, both at work and socially. Shiites make up a large proportion of the staff, including in the middle and higher echelons. They are only excluded from the most senior positions.

In many regards the compound of Saudi Aramco (the official name is 'Saudi Arabian Oil Company') is a Western enclave in the Middle East, despite being situated in the most conservative country in the entire region.

Different standards prevail here than elsewhere in the kingdom, with individual qualities counting for more than family or tribal connections. People work hard, talent is recognised and rewarded, and expertise is fostered. Saudi Aramco is by far the most rationally based and efficiently run company in Saudi Arabia.

It is a 'state within the state', says a leading executive in Aramco's Entrepreneurship Center. 'It is one of the king's instruments for getting things done which would otherwise be impossible. In this way he not only manages to steer clear of opposition from reactionary forces in his own government, but also from that of the conservative clerics.' He cites examples in the field of education, sport and employment opportunities. Within these projects people are not subjected to the 'Bedouin mentality' to which the government itself, as he points out, is also not immune.

The well-known Shiite philosopher Tawfiq al-Saif confirms this picture, but goes a step further in his assessment of the autonomy of Saudi Aramco:

It is without exception the dominant power in the Eastern Province and it is managed with the utmost efficiency. Most government bodies work at cross-purposes to each other and are therefore grossly inefficient. Saudi Aramco stands alone; it has a gigantic budget and sometimes pursues a policy that is at odds with the king's own wishes, for instance with regard to land-use policy. You can't really say that the king runs the firm.

It is not hard to find critics of this separate status. The Aramco official we interviewed explains, 'You have two camps in Saudi Arabia. Take for instance how people view our CEO, Khaled al-Falih. They either love him or hate him. Personally I think he is super!' That not everyone shares his affection for al-Falih was spectacularly demonstrated in August 2012 when hackers used the malware Shamoon to break into the firm's computer network. An obscure group, the Cutting Sword of Justice, succeeded in paralysing 30,000 of the company's computers, without however seriously endangering its oil production. The group accuses the Saudi authorities of 'crimes and atrocities' in Syria and Bahrain. Saudi Aramco is no 'island', as is often averred. In their view, it is a direct extension of the Saud family.

4

THE TICKING TIME BOMB

THE SOARING AMBITIONS OF THE NEW GENERATION

'It is time to listen to Saudi youth'—this was the heading of an op-ed in the *Saudi Gazette*.[1] It was a *cri de coeur* about the huge problem of the disproportionately large number of young people in Saudi Arabia. The Arab Spring has highlighted this issue yet again. It was indeed the younger generation that made up the greater part of the jam-packed squares in various Arab capitals calling for the fall of the regime. After the initial euphoria, these youthful revolutionaries have experienced little but disappointments. The fact that the younger generation was present en masse was not in itself surprising, because the Middle East has a very young population—the youngest in the world after Africa.

Two-thirds of the indigenous population in Saudi Arabia are under thirty.[2] In the coming ten to twenty years this will present the country with considerable economic, social and possibly political problems. Between 1950 and 2013 the population has expanded from 3 million to around 30 million—a tenfold increase. The demographic profile is unlikely to change in the coming period; the average age will stabilise at around thirty, but only by 2026.[3] In other words, by then 'merely' half the population will be under thirty. To what extent does this youth boom pose a serious threat to stability?

Poverty in the country of black gold

At first sight there does not seem to be many clouds on the horizon. Saudi Arabia has huge oil reserves—the second largest in the world (after Venezuela)—and due to the reasonably high price of oil in the period between 2005 and 2014 the national monetary reserves rose to around $750 billion in 2014.[4] In 2013 the state earned $274 billion from oil exports.[5] Enormous sums like this, however, do not mean very much in themselves. In terms of gross domestic product per capita Saudi Arabia ($31,245) is lagging behind neighbouring states such as Qatar ($98,814), Kuwait ($39,706) and Bahrain ($34,584).[6]

A sizable part of the state revenues is siphoned off by the secret but undoubtedly colossal expenses of the royal family, which has proliferated to around 7,000 or 8,000 princes and princesses, all of whom receive a monthly allowance varying from a couple of thousand to more than $250,000.

Defence outlays, which are also guarded by secrecy, account for a similarly large slice of the revenues from oil. According to the estimates of the Stockholm International Peace Research Institute (SIPRI) Saudi Arabia has spent 8 to 10 per cent of its gross domestic production on the military in recent years. It is a percentage that makes it the number one country in the world; per head of the population, it amounts to more than double the comparable figure spent by the United States and Russia, and is almost five times as much as Great Britain, France and China.[7]

Although there are hardly any official figures available, it is a well-known fact that there is a dramatic inequality of incomes in Saudi Arabia. While the average income per head of the population in 2013 was around SR8,000 ($3,133) a month, a large number of inhabitants have to get by with a much lower income. With the average family in Saudi Arabia amounting to six members, this is barely enough for many people to enjoy a decent existence. It is true that healthcare and education are free, although both these services are frequently of a poor quality, while water, electricity and petrol are heavily subsidised. For many Saudis life is an everyday struggle to make ends meet.

Is there such a thing as genuine poverty in Saudi Arabia, the country of black gold and skyscrapers gleaming in the sun? Estimates vary and there are no precise figures, but a considerable number of Saudis have a problem just getting by.[8] According to the statistics of the Ministry of Social Services the poverty line is at SR1,800 ($480) a month. One leading economist at the King Fahd University of Petroleum and Minerals in Dhahran has made a calculation of his own. 'The government's figures are not really reliable. I reckon that 35 per cent of the population has to get by with much less than SR2,000 a month ($533). They are poor.' There are also 'genuinely' poor people who often have even less of an income. They do not just come from neglected provinces such as Asir, Jizan and Najran, but from the big cities as well. Al-Suwaidi, al-Jarradiyah and al-Shimaisi (in Riyadh) and al-Karantina, al-Rowais and al-Salamah (in Jeddah) are slums that rival each other in notoriety, inhabited not just by extremely poor Saudis but also by foreign workers, who live from charity or, in many cases, from crime. According to some sources the average foreign worker earns as little as 1,000 riyals ($266) a month.[9]

YouTube films have revealed the scale of destitution. 'We are being Cheated: Poverty in Saudi Arabia' interviews some desperately poor people in the slums of Riyadh and Jeddah.[10] This material was sensitive enough to get the film-makers put in jail a few weeks after their film went online. In the summer of 2013 a campaign was launched on Twitter under the hashtag 'Salary doesn't meet my needs'. In the first two weeks it got more than 10 million tweets. The popular activist Manal al-Sharif tweeted:

The government gives money interest-free to Egypt, Jordan and Tunisia and uses a third of the national budget to fund the Riyadh metro scheme. And all the while Saudis spend most of their salaries on rent, private schools and private hospitals—the public ones often being of inferior quality.[11]

Plenty of graduates for very few jobs

Let us return to the younger generation. 'We're lazy,' explains a twenty-two-year-old student of English in Jeddah when the problem of the enormously high youth unemployment is raised. 'We let foreigners do the work that we are not prepared to do.' Three students of political science at the King Saud University in Riyadh all say the same thing: 'There's something wrong with our work ethic. This leads to "voluntary unemployment."

Many young people are spoiled by their families and the education they get doesn't do much to change that.' There is an increasing realisation that Saudis must start rolling up their sleeves. Maybe it is only occurring piecemeal, but you come across increasing numbers of Saudi men in posts you did not see them occupy five or ten years ago—such as taxi driver, hotel receptionist, cashier, bank clerk, in Mobily telephone shops or serving lattes at Starbucks. Women too are becoming more and more visible on the shop floor. Amid the gold bras and pink panties in the lingerie shops you currently see Saudi shop assistants, wearing niqabs and clad from top to toe in their abayas. It is questionable, however, whether anything has really changed. Given the unemployment statistics, this issue is as urgent as ever, as is the need for a reversal of current economic policy and for greater job opportunities in the private sector.

The official figure for unemployment in 2012 was 10.9 per cent; the real figure may have been considerably higher. A senior ARAMCO official who wants to remain anonymous does not trust government statistics. 'The real figure for unemployment lies closer to 27 to 29 per cent.' More alarming still is the fact that most jobseekers are between twenty and twenty-nine years old. Almost 40 per cent of those aged between twenty and twenty-four are unemployed. A disproportionately high number of them are women—an average of half the young female jobseekers fail to find work. The participation of women in the labour market is among the lowest in the Middle East, with 12 per cent employed.[12] Every year the universities turn out between 250,000 and 300,000 graduates (slightly more women than men) who are looking for work but are increasingly unable to find it.[13] The same is also largely true of the already overpopulated public sector where nine out of ten working Saudis end up. The private business community, where nine foreigners work for one Saudi, shows little interest in these employees who are barely qualified, if at all.

Extra obstacles are placed in the path of women. The separation between men and woman requires expensive alterations to the shop floor which by no means all employers are willing to implement. More generally, the educational system should be blamed, in addition to the widespread distaste for manual labour or domestic work, even though a great many unemployed Saudis are not really qualified for much else. A large majority of those who have university degrees or diplomas graduated in 'soft' subjects such as religious studies, sociology or Islamic history. They enter the job market totally unprepared. According to Abdullah Dahlan, who runs a professional training institute in Jeddah, '82 per cent of university students graduate in faculties that are totally irrelevant to the economy.'[14] It is a much-debated issue on Twitter. @essamz, for instance, remarks that 'When enormous numbers of students are graduating in literary and religious disciplines, who is going to help build up the economy?' In short, many Saudis are not qualified for the jobs they want to have and they refuse to accept the ones for which they do have the qualifications.

The Arab uprisings have forced the government to take account of this ticking time bomb. Ever since the mid-1990s attempts have been made to institute a 'Saudisation policy', but so far these efforts have got bogged down in bureaucratic buck-passing between the different ministries, resistance from the private sector and fraudulent visa applications. A hilarious case of the latter was when the princely governor of the Eastern Province granted 3,000 work permits to a friend and business colleague, just as he was about to give a speech at a Saudisation conference. In recent years the government has issued increasing numbers of visas for foreign workers under pressure from the business world; between 2005 and 2011 the number doubled, with 2.5 million visas issued.[15]

Continuing dependence on a foreign workforce

Recently it would seem as though the problem is being tackled more seriously. Since 2011 various programmes have been launched, such as *Hafiz* (Stimulus) and *Liqaat* (Encounter), with the aim of linking employers with jobseekers, complemented with training schemes and supported by a system of unemployment benefits to a maximum of €400 a month. The vast majority (85 per cent) of the applications for these allowances were by women.

The programme that has caused the most stir is called *Nitaqat* (Zones) and was started in September 2011. It consists of a complicated system of labels ('blue' or 'premium', 'green', 'yellow' and 'red') which private sector companies are allocated according to the quota of Saudis in their labour force that they are expected to employ. The aim is to raise the number of

Saudis from 10 per cent to an average of 36 per cent depending on the category of the firm. With banks that employ more than 500 people, for instance, the percentage is 49. For other businesses, such as lingerie shops, 100 per cent Saudi staff is obligatory. Anyone who has more foreigners on its books than they are permitted must pay a fine.

To put it politely, the implementation of the *Nitaqat* programme has not exactly gone smoothly. In business circles, where managers feel seriously hampered in their freedom to attract suitable staff, there has been a particular degree of resentment:

'Why should I pay the price for a decrepit educational system?' complains one Saudi businessman. 'If the state requires me to take on Saudis, then they should first of all give them a decent training. I am investing to make a profit, not to paper over the cracks in government policy.'[16]

In the spring of 2013 panic broke out in some business sectors because many foreigners, who had been taken on illegally or else not via the proper 'sponsors', were afraid of being arrested and did not show up for work. At the end of March that year three-quarters of the small telephone shops in Riyadh remained closed and port activities in Jeddah were paralysed because eight out of ten workers failed to show up.

The papers spoke of a pending exodus of 'two to three million illegal workers', something that provoked the generally not particularly empathetic Grand Mufti Abd al-Aziz Al al-Sheikh to appeal for 'mildness and friendliness towards foreign workers'.[17] The ministry felt constrained to introduce a temporary relaxation of the measures that had been announced—until the beginning of November 2013. In September the Ministry of Employment announced that in the preceding months 800,000 illegal foreigners had already been deported.[18] At the beginning of November 2013 some 5 million 'unregulated' migrant workers had had their situation regularised and a million had departed freely or been deported.[19] In the following months the number of deportations continued at the same level—in the last two months of 2013 and January 2014 'more than a quarter of a million' foreign workers were deported.[20] In late 2014 it was reported that almost 86 per cent of companies and establishments were in a *Nitaqat* safe zone.[21]

At the same time, Labour Minister Adel al-Fakeih announced that Saudi Arabia had doubled the number of its citizens working for private companies since it introduced the reforms to tackle long-term unemployment. What deserved special attention, according to the minister, was that three times as many women are employed in the private sector as in the period before the *Nitaqat* programme. The latter occurred in the teeth of opposition from conservative elements in the clergy. Some hawks in this sector even tweet about the minister that they 'wish him cancer, the same illness that his predecessor Ghazi al-Gosaibi died of'.[22]

There are, however, some more progressive voices. Prince Al-Waleed bin Talal, for instance, says he will be only too happy if more women find employment outside the home. In the same spirit, women should be permitted to drive. He regularly sends tweets with this sort of message: 'In order to abolish illegal work the correct decision is to allow women to drive. This will lead to at least 500,000 fewer foreign chauffeurs, and will be economically and socially advantageous for the nation.'

It has yet to be seen whether the Saudisation programme will create enough jobs to reduce youth unemployment to any extent. It depends on a cocktail of factors which might also incline one to doubt whether it will succeed in the longer term—high birth rates (admittedly these have fallen considerably since the beginning of this century, but the population is still growing at more than 1.5 per cent a year),[23] an inadequate educational system, the aversion to manual or domestic labour, the taboo on women's employment that is only slowly being eroded and a rigid, capital-intensive economy. In the short term, it is perhaps the private sector itself that is the biggest obstacle. Many businessmen are addicted to cheap foreign labour and a number of companies would fail if they were forced to take on large numbers of more expensive Saudis. They thus do their utmost to find a way round the excessively draconian measures of the *Nitaqat* programme. One businessman in al-Khobar confesses, 'I have to take on illegal workers, because otherwise I can't compete with the big companies. After all, they have *wasta* [contacts], enabling them to do what they want.'

One of the dodges used most frequently is 'Fake Saudisation' (*sawda wahmiah*), which involves putting 'phantom employees' on the payroll— the company takes on a certain number of Saudis (based on the *Nitaqat* quotas), sometimes even members of their own family, and pays them a salary to stay at home.[24] An employee of Rolex in Jeddah explains:

Our company regularly puts Saudi women on the payroll—with the striking fact that five women are worth as much as ten men—and asks them, whatever else they do, not to come to work. In general, my manager wants as few Saudis as possible on the shop floor—they don't work hard enough, they are totally undisciplined and they often leave after a few weeks.

In this way the firm still qualifies for the 'green' or even the 'premium' zone of the *Nitaqat* programme with all the pertaining advantages—among them the permission to continue to attract foreign labour. Economists such as John Sfakianakis assume that a large number of foreign workers will still be employed in the kingdom in the coming period.[25] In 2013, for instance, 1,700,000 employment visas were issued.[26]

Increasing frustration

In the wake of the Arab Spring King Abdullah launched his programme of hand-outs, worth billions, an important part of which consisted of the creation of 126,000 jobs in the public sector, plus the setting of a minimum wage and a bonus of two months' salary for civil servants. All this was aimed at keeping his subjects happy and off the streets. Now that oil prices have fallen substantially since mid-2014 it is increasingly questionable whether his successor will remain able to offer enormous hand-outs like this—unless he is prepared to tap into the financial reserves. In the long run, it seems hardly credible that the government will be able to placate people, particularly because of the ever-growing problem of youth unemployment. 'At the end of the decade, there will be more than 2.5 million Saudis looking for jobs,' claims John Sfakianakis.[27]

When young men have no job at all or one with a miserable salary, it means that they have problems finding a suitable fiancée. In recent years it is not just the expenses of a wedding that have soared, but fathers are also constantly asking bigger marriage portions for their better-educated daughters. In 2009 that led among other things to an online protest by a group of angry men under the caption, 'Let her become an old maid, if that's what she wants.' Abdel Rahman, a twenty-year-old in Riyadh with a scanty salary as a desk clerk in a shopping centre, complains about this sort of marriage issue. 'This will never work out properly and I can only hope for the best. If nothing changes in my situation, I'm afraid that my sweetheart will marry someone else.'[28] For a few years now wedding ceremonies held for a number of couples simultaneously have been organised and financed by a charity, a rich businessman or someone from the royal family in order to reduce the costs of a wedding.

And that is not all. Another problem is that when Saudis marry they are expected to own their own home. Affordable living accommodation is scarce, so much so that only a third of families have a house or flat of their own. It is true that half way through 2012 a new mortgage law was passed making it easier to buy a house, but this is thought to be insufficient. 'This law should have been passed a hundred years ago,' says a businessman in al-Khobar; he is joking, but he is also angry. Marriages are therefore postponed indefinitely—a special term has been coined for this situation, 'waithood'—and frustration builds up both among men and women.

There is plenty of criticism about dirty tricks around the ownership of land which could be made available for building desperately needed affordable homes. Immense tracts of uncultivated land were donated in the past by the royal family to influential friends or are still owned to this day by one or other of the princes. These friends then did nothing with the land, beyond putting a fence round it or using it for speculation—they do not have to pay taxes on it. It is a controversial subject that provokes plenty of indignation, including on Twitter. The popular term for this practice is *shabuk* (iron meshing) and it infuriates the countless people on housing waiting lists. Their frustration finds various outlets, the high point being the short film *Monopoly* that went viral on YouTube and was watched 750,000 times in the week it was launched, a figure that rose to 2 million in 2014.[29] Among other things, the film contains a portrait of a young man who spends his days in (and on top of) a van, waiting philosophically for a house that will never come.

At the beginning of 2011 King Abdullah launched a plan for the construction of 500,000 homes,[30] but whether these will be affordable is yet to be seen. In any case, thirty-four-year-old Amjad Turkistani does not have much faith in the project:

We really wish to own a house but prices remain high, mortgages are hard to come by and financial loans are difficult to find. Therefore, many of us are still renting. I have been married for four years with two kids and till this date have not been able to afford to buy a house because of high prices and difficult demands by local banks in order to get a loan. Even getting a personal loan through friends and members of the family is also becoming hard.[31]

In as much as there is any talk of protest by the younger generation, it occurs for the most part via social media and the issue is one of material conditions rather than the lack of political freedom or civil rights. The latter are more of an issue with Saudis in their thirties or forties.[32] Young people are mostly concerned with the lack of jobs and the shortage of housing. Students also complain about inadequate university facilities, incompetent teachers and ubiquitous corruption. For instance, in Abha, in the south-west of the country, serious disturbances occurred at King Khaled University on a number of occasions. In the spring of 2012 the female students succeeded in bringing about the dismissal of the university president. Similar protests took place, also by female students, at Tabuk University, in the far north-west of the country. Spectacular images of thousands of women students demonstrating, dressed in abayas, were circulated on Facebook and YouTube.

'We don't suffer enough'

Even if some of the young, both of orthodox and liberal persuasions, are politically active, this occurs online and only occasionally offline. What is striking is that most of them have little or no interest in politics in general. Perhaps the most important factor underlying this political apathy was the popularity of King Abdullah. Hardly less relevant is the widely shared notion that the House of Saud is the cement that holds the country together. If people want political change they do not want it by way of revolution. They are much too attached to the creature comforts of everyday security and peace, and this attitude is only reinforced by the chaos, the bloodshed and economic malaise that Iraq, Yemen, Bahrain, Egypt and Syria are suffering.

A twenty-four-year-old doctor in Jeddah, Rayan Karkadan, says that the average Saudi leads a more comfortable life than his contemporaries in

Egypt and Tunisia. 'We have too much to lose; we don't suffer enough.' His colleague of the same age, Obai al-Bashir, confirms this, 'We're afraid to leave our comfort zone behind.'

Religion too has a subduing effect on political activism. Muhammad, a student of political science at the King Saud University in Riyadh, expresses this eloquently, 'It is right for political parties to remain illegal; they are aiming to take power after all and that's not something we want here! We should treat the king with proper respect.' It goes without saying that fear plays a role—the shadow of arbitrary arrests and long prison sentences, often coupled with months of solitary confinement, that political dissidents face, hangs over everyone. It was mainly due to fear that the Day of Rage on 11 March 2011 was a total flop.

Things can of course suddenly get out of hand. One only needs to look at the revolts in the early days of the Arab Spring which nobody had predicted. Virtually nobody, however, expects the Saudi government to be confronted with angry and rebellious young people on a massive scale, no matter how frustrated they are with their social situation.

On the other hand, it is difficult to imagine this situation continuing indefinitely. The increasing contact of young Saudis with other cultures, especially through the information revolution on the Internet, will have an exponential influence on them (see Chapter 7, 'The Digital Explosion'). Soon the royal family will undergo a crucial transition, with princes from the second and third generation of the Saud family competing for power. A situation like this may create space for critical voices in society, because it is only to be expected that one or more princes will seek popular support to head off the competition. 'Otherwise,' an activist sighed, 'we will have thirty more years of dictatorship until the situation simply explodes, and God help us when that happens.'[33]

Another factor that will play a role in the coming years is the return of the tens of thousands of students who have studied abroad in the context of King Abdullah's scholarship programme. They will not only return armed with their degrees but most of them will also have spent their time in a totally different political and cultural environment. The first wave, numerically still rather modest, has already returned, but soon there will be a second and a third wave coming back with their degrees and almost certainly failing to find any proper employment and thus unable to afford a house or get married. If, moreover, the social restrictions have not been reduced and there is no more political freedom, these will be sufficient ingredients for a large-scale protest. Nobody will be taken in any longer by financial hand-outs, such as those the king issued early in 2011. Some young people are already expressing their reservations:

We need a long-run plan to improve the incomes. And we don't want to stay waiting for a grant, a gift. No, we need something that we deserve … And if the government doesn't give me these things, I will not be silent. I will not accept it anymore.[34]

Expectations such as these can only increase over time.

5

CHANGES BEHIND THE VEIL

WOMEN ON THE MOVE

Everyone agrees that Saudi Arabia is changing, but opinion is divided as to whether the changes are fundamental or merely superficial. Are they lasting, or might Abdullah's successor, or another monarch, reverse them? And are the majority of women, let alone men, in favour of change? There is no consensus on any of these issues.

The backward situation of women in the kingdom is almost a cliché. What everyone knows about Saudi Arabia is that women are not allowed to drive cars and are hidden from men as much as possible. They are all clad in the abaya, preferably in combination with a niqab as far as the religious police are concerned. They are thought of as anonymous black ghosts who sneak around the white marble shopping centres, or as second-class citizens who have to ask their male guardian for permission for every decision of any importance. All this is largely true, but often enough it is not entirely the case. The state of women's rights serves as a good barometer for Saudi society.

In retrospect it is easy to see the extent of the changes that have taken place. Over fifty years ago Crown Prince Faisal opened the first public school for girls in Saudi Arabia, despite fierce opposition from influential ultra-conservative clerics backed by public opinion. His argument was that nobody was forcing anyone to send their daughters to school. To meet their objections, he entrusted the organisation and supervision of girls' education to the religious establishment. The clergy saw it as their task to turn out god-fearing women who would see to the needs of their husbands and children and run the household. The family is after all one of the cornerstones of Islam.

This limited concept of education for girls belongs to the past. Saudi Arabia remains an extremely conservative society, but the distrust the population then felt with regard to the education of their daughters has totally disappeared. There are more women studying at (women's) universities than there are men at (men's) universities. The clergy have been stripped of their say over education for girls, and the deputy minister of education is a woman, the first to hold cabinet office. 'No family today is opposed to the notion of its daughters studying and working,' says Nora (seventeen), who is taking her finals at one of the private schools in Riyadh. She plans to study graphic design after which she will maybe start a business. Another Nora, who is also seventeen and who is preparing to go abroad to study fashion, endorses her, 'All Saudis have changed.' But at the end of the day, when they leave school through the double doors that protect them from curious male eyes, the female guards make sure they are wearing face-veils.

Grandmothers

The separation between men and women was not always implemented so strictly. The grandmother of the historian Hatoon Ajwad al-Fassi was educated in different times:

In the countryside the women shared the work with the men. On the farms they had to milk the cows and work on the land and go to the market. Even when they were at home on their own they were strong. My grandmother had no objection to allowing male visitors to enter her house. She was strong and had plenty of self-confidence. This was a reflection of how society viewed women.

This was not only the case in the countryside. Many Saudi interviewees recall grandmothers who were much more independent and nothing like 'the dead meat', the label that one Saudi psychologist uses to describe many of her contemporaries. These grandmothers grew up in another atmosphere. Newspapers then carried advertisements for night clubs in Jeddah. This city qualifies as much more liberal than Riyadh, but night clubs are long since a thing of the past, even there.

Everything changed in 1979. It was the year of the Islamic revolution in the Shiite neighbouring state of Iran, of the Soviet invasion of Afghanistan and of the occupation of the Grand Mosque in Mecca by Juhayman's fanatics who took a stand against 'the degeneration of Islamic norms'.

The occupation of the Grand Mosque was quashed with much bloodshed, but the government then implemented an Islamic revolution of its own in order to restore its tarnished prestige. This was the reason underlying the tightening up of public norms which were savagely enforced by the religious police.

'We discovered that things gradually started being forbidden,' Hatoon al-Fassi said a couple of years ago. 'We heard about the rules restricting our behaviour and then we noticed that they had become institutionalised. Restaurants are a good example. In the 1970s they were open for everyone. But then they started creating separate rooms for families. We learned that women were sometimes no longer allowed in them. First of all they told us informally that this was how it was; later on we saw the signs on the door. Towards the 1990s new restaurants were obliged to have a separate section for women, a sort of cubicle. This then became the norm, with the result that the mutawwa, the religious police, inspects the building plans before construction work is started.'

So today in Starbuck's in the centre of Riyadh only men are allowed to sit and chat comfortably on the outdoor terrace, while women have to sit indoors, in a sweaty sort of canteen, hidden behind frosted glass.

Segregation in Saudi Arabia is more drastically implemented than in any other state in the Islamic world, now that the even more conservative Taliban regime in Afghanistan has been ousted. Even so the separation of men and women who are not immediate family has never been carried out systematically. A nurse, Hana al-Awami, works in the operating theatre of a hospital alongside men, because in healthcare segregation is unattainable. The face-veil is forbidden. (Hana, who grew up wearing one, recalls how naked she felt when she had to take it off.) It is against public morality for actresses to appear live on stage with actors, but they are allowed to do so if a programme is being filmed for Saudi TV. Women are not allowed to drive cars, but they are permitted to sit unchaperoned in a car driven by a chauffeur. But then chauffeurs are always foreigners and they do not really count as 'men'.

It is not as if women are calling en masse for the relaxation of the rules governing women's dress or for the abolition of the system of male guardians or for permission to drive cars. On the contrary, the authorities can still claim a conservative majority that would reject reforms like these. While there are admittedly no statistics on the subject of change, if one asks young and even not so young women about it, they are by no means necessarily positive towards it. The pianist Nadine in Jeddah, who appears on YouTube films without a headdress, is in favour of a religious police force, 'provided they comply with definite rules. They could tell everyone what the accepted social forms are.' Hana al-Awami, the nurse in the operating theatre, thinks it is strange that there are no cinemas in Saudi Arabia. Should they come, however, it would be better if they had separate days for men and women.

Hana herself would dearly like to drive a car. Hatoon al-Fassi and Fawzia al-Bakr, a sociologist, were among the group of women who went and sat in the driving seat in 1990 in the centre of Riyadh, paying the price for a long time with their careers. But there are also highly educated women who do not call for this change at all. Bshayea and Reem, who are psychology students at the huge Princess Nora University in Riyadh, say that they would not even dare to drive. Every time some women take the step of sitting in the driving seat, as has happened with some frequency since 2011, countless people, including women, have criticised them on Twitter.

In 2009 the great debate began for the relaxation—specifically not the abolition—of the strict separation between men and women. It began with the opening of the first university where men and women can study together—the King Abdullah University for Science and Technology near Jeddah. The mixed university, better known under its English acronym KAUST, is one of King Abdullah's pet projects. The opening of KAUST made a profound impression on professor of educational psychology,

Fawzia al-Bakr. 'For the first time I had the experience of a Saudi woman speaking to a mixed audience. The king was seated with the rectors of all the universities, including those of Mecca and Medina, in the front rows; even ultra-conservative men were present at this event!'

Al-Bakr thought that the king had been exceptionally courageous:

The segregation between men and women is a very sensitive question in Saudi Arabia; it is the underlying cause of all the tensions in society, religion, in the labour market and in education, you name it. Society is made up of men and women. If there is a problem in the way they relate, the whole of society stagnates. And that is precisely what has happened here.

The debate really flared up in December of that year when Sheikh Ahmad Qassim al-Ghamdi announced in an interview in the newspaper *Okaz* that the segregation between men and women has no basis in Islamic law, as long as women were correctly clad in the abaya and veil. At the time al-Ghamdi was the head of the mutawwa in the holy city of Mecca, which meant that many people took his pronouncement very seriously.

Others, however, condemned him straightaway. He was invited to take part in a TV debate in which some of his fellow clerics shouted him down. The press announced his dismissal, while another leading cleric, Sheikh Abd al-Rahman al-Barrak, called for the death of everyone who advocated heresies of this sort. Direct contact between the sexes leads after all to a 'view of what is forbidden and to forbidden conversations between men and women'.

A second TV debate was held, in which al-Ghamdi did get a chance to speak and where his supporters were able to phone in. He also announced in the press that nobody had told him he had been dismissed—this was shorthand for the fact that he enjoyed protection in the highest circles.

A year later the Arab Spring put an abrupt end to the debate on change. The whole gamut of restrictions was tightened up once more to keep the revolution at bay. Enormous investments in job opportunity programmes were accompanied by a ban on demonstrations. Speaking in the name of the government, the clergy declared all protest to be in conflict with Islam. The subject of 'change' became taboo. Al-Ghamdi lost his job after all and KAUST never really got off the ground. In her blog 'Saudiwoman's

Weblog', the blogger Eman al-Nafjan wrote that the government had come up with a marvellous invention—a time machine it could use to restore the whole country to the notorious 1980s.[1]

Women in the Shura

Was it King Abdullah's admittedly cautious openness to reform or the pressure from social media and satellite TV? In any case, in contrast to what happened in the 1980s and 1990s, the movement for change soon started up again. In September 2011 the king announced that he intended to appoint thirty women to his advisory council, the Majlis al-Shura. Furthermore, women were granted suffrage in the local elections to be held in 2015.

These were definitely the most important changes since Crown Prince Faisal opened the first public school for girls in 1960, even if the Shura is only an advisory body and elections in Saudi Arabia have not exactly had much impact so far. For the first time in forty years elections were held in 2005—for half of the members of municipal councils. There was, however, not much interest in them and only 18 per cent of enfranchised males in Riyadh cast their votes. As far as is known the turnout for the local elections in 2011 was also very low. Moreover, it is not at all clear what these councils are supposed to do. That a change has occurred, however, with Saudi women acquiring an extra right, is undeniable.

In his address to the Shura the king explained that his decision was entirely in conformity with sharia law. Islamic women, he said, have given their opinions and advice ever since the time of the Prophet Muhammad. 'We refuse,' he said, 'to marginalise women in society in their roles that comply with the Islamic Shariah.'[2]

The grand mufti, the principal religious mainstay of the monarchy, was present at the session of the Shura to applaud the king's decision. Yet his backing was anything but heartfelt; in 2006 he attributed the case for giving women the franchise and other rights to Christians and Jews who wanted to destroy Islam. A few months before the king gave women the suffrage, the grand mufti expressed his displeasure about a citizen's petition to the king requesting equal rights for women. 'Do demands like this serve Islam?' was his rhetorical question.

With the occasional exception, the ultra-conservative clergy is opposed to all change. They maintain that Islam already guarantees women equal rights. Women are cherished as mothers, spouses and daughters; their role is complementary to that of the man. Anyone who disputes this is guilty of a corrupt interpretation of the faith. Clerics never tire of informing us on Twitter that change is bound to lead to free sex and gay marriage. Sheikh Abd al-Rahman al-Barrak—it was he who had so savagely denounced his colleague al-Ghamdi—emphasises that 'equality can only exist between things that are identical'. He went on to add that 'God has differentiated between men and women in the sharia of islam, required by their nature and legacy.'[3]

Shopping

One of the most effective promoters of the cause of women has been a man—Khalid al-Khudair, who set up a recruitment agency for women at the end of 2011:

As a man I had great difficulty finding work. Not because there is no work, but because companies don't invest in a proper staffing policy. If I had problems as a man, it is obvious that it must have been all the more difficult for a woman. My sister couldn't even get an interview with the personnel department. She had to hand her CV over to the security personnel. I wanted to start something which would have a lasting impact on society, just to show that you could take on the most difficult challenges and still succeed.

A relatively large number of Saudi women are active in the top echelons of the business world. They own about 40 per cent of family firms, even if they are often just silent partners. They are worth 21 per cent of all private investments, while at the same time there is high unemployment among ordinary women. According to official statistics, 34 per cent of Saudi women were out of work in 2013.[4] Economic necessity moreover is an important motor of change.

By a fortunate coincidence, al-Khudair's initiative occurred at the same time as the government's decision to allow women to work in lingerie shops. This was something that had been discussed for years, but the clergy had always been able to put a spanner in the works. Women were not allowed to work in shops, as it offended proper morality, even though it was not considered immoral for Indian or Bengali men to sell women's bras and panties. The Shura, however, made the opening move and the new minister of labour, Adel al-Fakeih, won the support of the king, which was necessary to bypass the outraged clergy.

Al-Khudair's company is called 'Glowork, Glowing Careers for Women'— its colours are pink and grey, which are 'not normal here, so they attracted attention'. He approached the Labour Ministry, pointing out that a billion dollars were being spent on unemployment benefits every month. 'Why shouldn't we become partners?' he asked. 'We put unemployed women on the market and we support them for a year. For this, you should pay us 10 per cent of their benefit.' To employers he said, 'I'll select your staff and train them for a year for nothing.'

He started with the lingerie shops and then transferred his attention to the cosmetics sector. Today women are also employed as cashiers in supermarkets. Al-Khudair's next speciality was abaya shops and furniture stores. 'Perceptions have changed. People see the positive side. First of all the business world was opposed because their firms had to be converted to keep men and women separate. Now it is very enthusiastic about this development, because women are good workers and profits are rising.'

By helping women to work, al-Khudair is chipping away at the harshest aspects of segregation. A separate entrance for men and women is no longer a requirement. Glowork's office staff also includes women. At the major business conferences that he organises men and women are no longer kept separate but mingle with each other.

'We try and change tradition, not religion. The tradition is for women not to work.' But this is changing rapidly. According to al-Khudair, the same number of women found jobs in 2012 as in the three years before that. And he promises that the entire shopping sector will become female. 'That will deliver 400,000 to 500,000 jobs over the next three years.' On 4 April 2014 the English-language Saudi newspaper *Arab News* announced that the number of Saudi women employed in the business community had risen from 42,400 in 2011 to 454,300 in 2013.[5] What is more, these figures were published in the context of an article about the high number of women who had given up their jobs in lingerie and other shops in the same sector due to the wages being so low.

Among his other activities, al-Khudair organises enormous job fairs for women. In 2013 17,000 jobseekers showed up for the first of these, held in Riyadh; in April 2014 the number rose to 20,000. More than ninety firms took part in the two-day meeting. Interested parties were taught how to write a CV and prepare for a job interview, skills that young Saudis in general do not possess.

The country is going through an enormous change, says al-Khudair. But how lasting is it? He quotes the model of King Abdullah's scholarship system:

Some 150,000 young Saudis are now studying abroad, of whom 30,000 are women, in countries from America to China. When they return they will know how things work elsewhere. They will have become more broad-minded as a result. They will understand the benefit of equal rights for men and women.

And he is by no means the only one to make this point. 'Even families with a conservative background now allow their daughters to go abroad and study,' says Dr Hind al-Sheikh, director of the Institute of Public Administration in Riyadh. 'Soon there will be someone who has studied abroad in every home. This will have a huge impact on society.'

Al-Khudair, with his infectious optimism, ducks questions about resistance from conservative quarters, although this has certainly not gone away. A conservative Saudi writer, Abdullah al-Dawood, urged his followers on Twitter to assault cashiers in supermarkets. When he saw the outrage that his tweet provoked, al-Dawood said that he had been misquoted. He did, however, mention a fatwa forbidding women from working as cashiers. This was followed by another cleric, Khalid Ibrahim al-Saqabi, who endorsed al-Dawood's original remarks.[6]

The resistance to change comes not just from the clergy but also from the middle ranks of the civil service. 'The ministers are very broadminded,' says Eman al-Nafjan in an interview in Riyadh. At the point of implementation, however, their decisions get blocked. 'Both the Ministry of Labour and the Ministry of the Civil Service have scrapped the requirement that a woman's guardian must give her permission if she wants to work for a company. All the same, companies continue to ask permission from the guardian,' says al-Nafjan. If they invest in a woman's training and her guardian decides to remove her, they cannot do anything about it. There is no law that can help her. 'There is a sort of *arrière garde* that just refuses to change. Look at the Ministry of Justice, how long did it take for the first female trainee lawyer? There's so much opposition to that idea.'

Samar Fatany, one of the first female radio journalists and a columnist in Jeddah, is similarly cautious. It is only due to the backing of King Abdullah that al-Khudair and the Minister of Labour Adel al-Fakeih have been able to achieve as much as they have. According to her, that is how things work in Saudi Arabia:

The king has given women new elbow room despite the resistance of aggressive opponents. He defies hawks and others who don't want to see any change. But will that remain the case when the king has gone? These opponents are still there, and even the king needs to be cautious in his dealings with them.

The blogger al-Nafjan agrees with Fatany that the king was defying the hawks:

He doesn't allow them to keep the power they used to have. When he appointed thirty women to the Shura the hawks went to the king and said, 'How can you do this?' They also constantly attack the Minister of Labour, telling him he is corrupting our women if they are allowed to work and that they will become immoral. The difference is that the government no longer listens to them. The decision allowing women to be shop assistants is a political decision. If the king supports it, it can't be ignored. If you get another king however who makes concessions to these hawks, all these advances will be reversed once more.

6

'EVERYONE HAS TO LEARN TO THINK FOR HIMSELF'

BILLIONS OF DOLLARS ARE SPENT ON EDUCATION

Viewed from the inside, School 120 in north Riyadh does not look very different from any random secondary school. True, it is single-sex, just girls and young women, but they have worked equally hard at their end-of-the-year projects as any school students in a European country. The pupils in the top two classes are presenting their papers before they go on holiday. They have depicted the deadly hazards of smoking and the influence of eating chocolate on stress, and they have made films about other cultures, about life in Jordan or the United States, and about their own future as dentists or artists, or in the business world.

Awadif (seventeen) steps proudly forward—she was selected for the Young Leaders days organised by the authorities. 'They work on motivation,' she says. 'We have to treat each other, all of us, as future leaders. We learned to develop our leadership skills and mentality.' This is the new wind that has been blowing for a few years now in the Ministry of Education. 'We no longer want the pupils to repeat mindlessly what the teacher says. Everyone has to learn to think for himself,' an advisor to the minister said later. The teachers at School 120 also stress this:

The projects are intended to encourage pupils to think for themselves. You have to learn not to withdraw into yourself timidly, but to come up for yourself and state your views in uninhibited fashion. You have to be able to communicate with others and be capable of taking decisions independently.

The pupils choose their projects themselves; the teacher is there just to give advice.

There are, however, plenty of problems with Saudi education. A storm of criticism broke when it emerged that so many of the participants in the attacks of 9/11 were from Saudi Arabia. The school textbooks used for the religious knowledge classes—the most important subject on the curriculum—propagated hatred of infidels and dissidents, creating a fertile atmosphere for terrorist activities. Radical teachers and clerics manipulated the strict form of Islam that prevails in Saudi Arabia anyway and were thus able to recruit people for extremism. Pupils and students were generally encouraged to be uncritical and to repeat parrot-fashion what their teachers said, while creativity and any new ideas were suppressed. A great deal has changed since then, but even today young Saudis have no realistic picture of their own potential. They choose subjects that offer them no future and there is too much emphasis on religious studies. The curriculum does not relate to the requirements of the business world. This is why companies prefer to employ foreigners and why so many young Saudis cannot find work. This is all the more the case now that the civil service, the preferred employer for many of the young, no longer has all that many openings.

The Saudi authorities are only too willing to admit that there are problems with education in the country. A drastic alteration of school textbooks was implemented with the aim of driving out extremism. (This was only done, however, after the royal family itself became the target of Muslim extremist terrorism in 2003, which the government then quashed with great violence, combining long sentences with re-education programmes in the prisons.) In the schools, moreover, a preventive campaign for 'intellectual security' has been launched that stresses the need for tolerance, respect for others and independent thinking. Secondary school pupils are the main target group, because they are at the critical age where they can be influenced by extremists.

Lectures are given and pamphlets and books distributed in the schools. Dr Abd al-Rahman al-Hadlaq, who coordinated the Interior Ministry campaign, is putting pressure on headmasters, teachers and clergy. 'They are influential actors in our struggle, because a teacher has a hundred pupils and an imam a thousand faithful.' The big problem with Saudi education, according to former deputy minister of education, Prince Khalid al-Mashari Al Saud, is the teachers:

Many teachers, both men and women, have almost no qualifications. This is a serious problem. Teachers come from the colleges of education, which don't attract the best students. The best of them go on to study medicine, technology or computer studies. The others go to the colleges of education.

Students at the King Fahd University of Petroleum and Minerals in Dhahran say something similar. 'The religious universities allow anyone in. So you can imagine the sort of people who graduate there and end up in education!'

Prince Khalid, who is now the president of the education committee in the Shura, stressed that entry requirements at the colleges of education needed to be made stricter. 'The standard has to be raised. This will also have put positive pressure on prospective pupils and raise their level.'

Many female teachers were, in his words, mass-produced at a time when there was a huge demand for them with the new programme of public schools for girls. 'And we can't just give them the sack. We'll have to wait until they retire.'

Conservatism

Religion, the clergy and tradition—in short, conservatism—have also had a devastating influence. That is especially evident in the education of girls, but boys suffer too. Public education for girls has only existed since 1960. The launching of public schools for girls was Crown Prince Faisal's achievement, but his wife, Iffat, had already done the groundwork. Up until then some girls had had an informal religious education. They did not do much more than learn the Quran by heart, with the Islamic code of conduct being drummed into them. This was until they reached puberty, after which they stayed at home and got married. After all, girls whose only task was to be good housewives and god-fearing mothers to their children did not need more than that.

Not surprisingly, the clergy were totally opposed to the idea of public schools for girls and their opposition was largely shared by the population. Crown Prince Faisal, however, turned their own argument—that the most important task for women was motherhood—against them. He pointed out that better education would actually produce better mothers. According to some sources, he argued, the Quran did not deny education to women. On the contrary, 'God enjoins education on every Muslim man and woman.'[1]

Initially, however, Faisal did not make education for girls obligatory; instead he tried to take the wind out of the sails of the religious establishment by giving it the task of supervising it. As a result, girls were subjected to extremely strict rules, much more so than boys. They had to spend more hours in religious instruction and had fewer classes in languages or the sciences and they got no gym or sports training at all. They remained hidden behind massive walls—men were not permitted so much as a glimpse of them. The clergy did not have much money to spare for girls' education either, which meant that they were often taught in dilapidated premises.

In 2002 this combination of neglected school buildings and being hidden at all costs from the eyes of men led to the death of fifteen schoolgirls in a fire in a secondary school in Mecca. According to a report in *Newsweek*, a surreptitiously lighted cigarette started the blaze that led to panic among the 750 pupils.[2] The building was locked and the porter had left his post on an errand. The fire brigade tried to rescue the girls from the burning building, but the religious police prevented them from doing their work because many of the girls had left their headscarves behind in their panic. Some of them were even driven back into the smoke and flames.

The response was furious. The population's distrust of their daughters being educated was already a thing of the past. The behaviour of the mutawwa proved the last straw. Abdullah, at the time a crown prince, used the tragedy as a pretext to deprive the clergy of their authority over girls' education. In that sense the fire can be said to have given this cautious reformer an opportunity. The Education Ministry was given the responsibility for supervising girls' schools instead.

The strict physical separation between girls' and boys' education lasts from primary school to university almost without exception, but there is no longer any difference in the curriculum. Girls have more than made up for their late start in education and there are currently more women than men at universities. Since 2009, moreover, there has even been a female minister of state in charge of the department of women's education at the Ministry of Education, Nora al-Faiz. As a female university professor proudly remarked, this makes her the first woman in Saudi Arabia who must be addressed as 'Your Excellency'.

A social convention

In the schools for girls, the women's universities and the department of girls' education at the Ministry of Education, all the veils and headscarves are taken off, once indoors. But then no men enter these premises anyway. The only ones in the vicinity are the security personnel at the perimeter entrance where all women going in or out of the building are obliged to wear both the abaya and the veil. 'Our society doesn't accept men and women working in the same building,' says Deputy Minister al-Faiz, who is anything but an advocate of the abolition of gender segregation:

Women are expected to cover their heads. I feel more comfortable in my workplace when I can take my abaya off. When I meet my male colleagues, I have to put it on again and cover my hair. And of course I cover my hair even when I'm travelling abroad. Firstly, it's a social convention. Secondly, in view of our norms, we experience it as easier and more comfortable if we work separately. Ten or twelve years ago I was on a training programme in Denver. And all the women in the USA and Canada complained that men bothered them at their work. When they asked me about this I could answer that, thank God, that's not something I have to face.

This is the current situation then, especially in the education sector where the separation between men and women remains strictly observed (unlike, for instance, in the health sector and to an extent in the business world): 'We have closed circuit TV. In this way I can "meet" everyone in the ministry. It's as though I'm sitting at a desk with them. I can see everything and discuss everything with them. They can hear me plainly, but they can't see me,' says al-Faiz. So she does not have to wear an abaya.

The ministry admits that the quality of the teachers remains a serious problem. For a long time the demand for teachers was such that all applicants were taken on. This is no longer appropriate in an information economy, which is what Saudi Arabia is aiming to become. It is in this context that the *Tatweer* (reform) programme was introduced a few years ago—the King Abdullah bin Abd al-Aziz Project for the Development of Public Education for girls and boys. *Tatweer* consists of training schemes for teachers, modernisation of the curriculum and improvements to conditions in the schools. Billions of dollars will be spent on a programme whose main goal is to see that the uncritical drumming in of teaching material trotted out by submissive teachers becomes a thing of the past. The state of affairs at School 120 in Riyadh is a product of this policy. 'I am responsible for the choices I make,' one young teacher says. 'I'm the one who says "yes" or "no", including to my own father.'

All the girls in their final pre-university years have ideas about their future. Wadif wants to become a doctor and so does Nouf. Deema aims for a career in law, while her sister is a lawyer already. The other schoolgirls tease her, 'So you want to fight for women's rights, Deema; go on, admit it.'

School 120 is a public school, and there are about ten times as many of them as there are private schools. The Riyadh Schools, which educate pupils from kindergarten to secondary school level and beyond, is a privately funded system for boys and girls—who, it goes without saying, do their lessons in separate buildings. The principal is always a man. On the girls' side there is an American-language syllabus as well as the normal Arabic one. The reason pupils follow the former is that many private universities and courses in medicine are also currently taught in English. Reham, for instance, is going to the new, private Faisal University, where a business degree course has been introduced. A large number of pupils also want to go to universities abroad.

Sport

By 2013 sports activities for girls were officially permitted at the private schools. At the Riyadh Schools this had already been the case for many years, even if these activities take place literally and figuratively in secret. As one aspect of the steady but slow reforms in the kingdom, however, sports for women have been legalised. The issue of obesity plays a background role here as well, as young people in Saudi Arabia are among the plumpest in the world.[3]

Under heavy pressure from the International Olympic Committee, Saudi Arabia sent two women to the games in London in 2012, one modestly clad sprinter who lived and ran in the United States, and a judoka wearing a headscarf. According to the BBC, the king, the crown prince, the minister for foreign affairs and leading clerics had discussed this sensitive issue at great length.[4] Both women were eliminated in the first round.

A few months before the Games, Human Rights Watch quoted a teacher at a women's university in one of its reports, who said that the female rector had permitted the students to play basketball and table tennis four years previously, but that the sports hall was never used and the rector had been replaced during a 'reorganization', because she was judged 'too progressive'.[5] In this context, the new official policy for sports in private schools was without any question a sign of progress.

According to a spokesperson in the Ministry of Education, the decision issued from 'the teachings of our religion which permitted women to engage in activities of this sort in accordance with sharia law'.[6] If sport, however, is not in breach of sharia, why were girls in public schools not automatically allowed to participate in sports as well? The answer is that the authorities were afraid of the opposition from conservative quarters and it was abundantly clear that a big step like this could not be taken in one go. The more gradual approach was intended to give the ulama and the conservative sectors of the population time to get used to the notion of women taking part in these activities. The second step, taken in April 2014, consisted of an official request from the Shura to the Ministry of Education to consider introducing sport for girls in state schools as well. This would of course be done with the understanding that the Islamic rules for clothing and segregation would be strictly maintained. Nonetheless, the request led to a rare street protest by dozens of conservative Saudis who opposed this 'Westernisation'.

King Abdullah was behind many of the changes in the field of education such as the founding of the mixed university near Jeddah, KAUST. According to the former deputy minister of education, Prince Khalid al-Mashari, KAUST was definitely an example to be imitated:

If you ask whether we should introduce coeducation for girls and boys in secondary schools, adolescents, that is, I would have to answer in the negative, because this would lead to all kinds of problems. In the universities however the students are mature enough to limit their relations to their work and not to do anything else which would be forbidden. We have to develop our culture in such a way that you can avoid any negative consequences. In a society like ours in which we have a very rigid form of segregation, you can't suddenly start letting men and women mingle. People have to learn how to relate to each other. This development however is beginning to take place.

Five years have passed at the time of writing (early 2015), and while KAUST has not yet come to a standstill, it has not really made much progress either. It is not in the news very much. Some people think that the authorities deliberately keep it out of the public eye, so as not to provoke the conservatives. According to Eman al-Nafjan, nobody pays much attention to the university as long as it remains cut off from Saudi society.

Scholarships

Another of the king's special projects that has in fact been launched successfully was his ambitious programme to provide young Saudis with scholarships to study abroad after getting their first degree at a Saudi university. The underlying notion is that once they have become acquainted with life abroad they will return with new, more open-minded attitudes. The programme began a couple of years ago. Now there are around 150,000 to 200,000 Saudis—depending on whom you are speaking to— studying abroad with a scholarship. *Arab News* reported that 111,000 Saudis were studying in the United States in 2014.[7] The United Kingdom has welcomed more than 10,000.[8] In China there are around 3,000 Saudi students, reason for a Saudi professor to say jokingly that Saudi Arabia would end up being the country with the most Chinese speakers outside China.

More and younger Saudi women are now going abroad on one of these scholarships. Dr Hind al-Sheikh of the Institute of Public Administration says that everyone wants to get one of them. Even traditional families with a strict religious background allow their daughters to go abroad. Al-Sheikh is tremendously proud of her institute, which offers a postgraduate education. In 2013 there were 1,377 jobs on offer for the 156 graduates. It seems that unemployment is not an issue here. It proves, she says, that a good education offers women new opportunities. She sees Saudi Arabia as having reached a crossroads. Motivation is a key to change, and that is now present in abundance. An important factor here is that the young people of today also have parents who have had a good education; there are plenty of working mothers.

Nonetheless, the old mentality dies hard.

'These are cultural problems,' says Robert Lacey. 'I have a young Saudi friend with a successful business that installs high-speed Internet cables in office buildings. There is of course plenty of demand for them because of the boom in new offices. He can get plenty of Saudi technicians; this is traditional and respected work. But there are no university-educated Saudis to be found for the administrative posts; they refuse to work for anyone other than people from their own tribe. His senior executive went to him and said he'd got one of those new jobs with the Home Office Ministry, so he was leaving. And my friend asked him why. After all he would get only half the salary there. The man said that his father thought the post was more honourable; his father doesn't understand why he works so hard for a firm that is not owned by a member of his family. It is more honourable to work for the government and easier too, as civil servants get a pension. What's more, he said, he could start his own business in his spare time. Also there are ways to earn more money when you work for the state. For instance by selling visas to Saudis for foreign workers.'

On the way to Riyadh airport is the new Princess Nora University. It is strictly for women, and with its 45,000 students it is the largest women's university in the world. It is a vast complex of hundreds of buildings, including mosques and a university hospital. Five twenty-year-old psychology students at the university are determined to seize their chance to prove themselves. They are a good indication of the degree of progress Saudi Arabia has made in recent years. Their personal notions about matters such as women behind the driving wheel or wearing the veil are not all the same; some are in favour of these changes, others are against. The country is changing, they say, and that is a good thing. What they also want to stress, however, is that change should not take place in the form of the Arab Spring. 'Then things will only get worse,' says Maryam. 'Just look at Syria, but also at Egypt: it's one big mess.'

These students know that once they have got their degrees, they will go abroad with a King Abdullah scholarship, after which they will get a job. And they are confident that they are entitled to the same rights as men. Bshayea: 'The notion that men should have more rights than women is a mistaken interpretation of the faith. Our religion gives men and women equal rights.' None of them have any problem with working in the same space as men. 'As long as they respect you,' says Maryam.

In Jeddah, the journalist and activist for women's issues, Samar Fatany, warns us against too great expectations. Fatany has already been through a lot. When she was young there was a prevailing optimism about progress, which was shattered by the radicalisation that set in after 1979. When we interviewed her in 2013 she said that much depended on King Abdullah:

'I have mixed feelings. We'll have to see. King Abdullah has shown that he is a man of his word. He's done everything he has promised. He's stood up to the hawks and other people who were opposed to all change. But will that be the same when he's no longer here? Those elements that are against change haven't gone away. And even the king has to be cautious in his dealings with them. They still have plenty of influence, and that's a negative aspect.'

'On the other hand,' she adds, 'there is the younger generation, comprising almost 70 per cent of the population. There is a struggle going on currently between the hawks and the reformers, both of whom want to influence the youth and get them into their camp. A huge number of young people are now returning from studying abroad. I think this was an extremely wise move on the king's part. These young people had to be exposed to the world; they had to experience how people live in other cultures, instead of becoming isolated and indoctrinated with this extremist ideology that doesn't permit any tolerance or acceptance of other cultures.'

'The hawks in the government were the problem. Moderates such as us were marginalised. Before the present king came to the throne, women weren't allowed to go to conferences or have their photo in the national press. Women are now getting the chance to prove themselves.'

'House of Wisdom'

The King Abdullah University for Science and Technology, better known as KAUST, is a relatively free-thinking oasis in a kingdom that is otherwise strictly Islamic. Everything is permitted on the campus of this mixed-gender university—there is even a cinema, something that is unimaginable elsewhere. But like the Aramco compound and the extravagance of Prince al-Waleed bin Talal, KAUST is only the exception that proves the rules that prevail in Saudi Arabia. There is no evidence to show that the rest of the country will follow its example or that the segregation of the sexes is rapidly going to be diluted.

The only areas of desegregation in the country have been the health service and medical education. This has been the case for a long time and for purely practical reasons—there are simply not enough male and female staff in the health sector for men to treat and care for men or women for women. Women are also beginning to break through in the business community which has hitherto been a male world. In education, however, girls and boys and men and women are still kept strictly separate. Women study at women's universities, and men at men's. And when there is only a male lecturer available for a specific subject at a women's university, he has to give his lectures via closed-circuit TV to avoid seeing his students.

This is why the opening of KAUST on 23 September 2009 was such a breakthrough—it is the first university in Saudi Arabia where students of both sexes can study together in every discipline. Admittedly KAUST is only for MA or PhD students—it is thought that mixed-gender education at an earlier age leads to confusion, and this notion is also held by some of the supporters of this oasis.

KAUST, in the village of Thuwal, an hour's journey by car from the port city of Jeddah, was King Abdullah's special project. He opened the university himself on Saudi Arabia's national day in the presence of 3,000 guests, male and female. Among them was the Bengali Nobel Prize-winner Muhammad Yunus, founder of the Grameen Bank in Bangladesh that aims to encourage social development by means of microcredit. In his speech Yunus emphasised how important the emancipation of women is for the worldwide war on poverty.

The king called KAUST a 'new house of wisdom' and a 'beacon for peace, hope and reconciliation'.

'The university,' he said, 'will be at the service of the people of the kingdom and will be of benefit to all the peoples of the world in accordance with the teachings of the holy Koran, which explains that God created humanity in order that we should get to know each other.'

Despite the fact that KAUST was one of King Abdullah's most cherished projects, a bitter struggle with the clerics and other conservative groups preceded its founding, and the clash of ideologies continued even after the university was opened. A month after the opening, a leading cleric, Dr Sa'ad bin Nasser al-Shithri, delivered a savage attack on national TV on the grounds that it is a mixed-gender university. In his view, 'The mingling of the sexes is a cardinal sin and a great evil.' Al-Shithri went too far, however, and to the delight of more progressive Saudis he was forced to resign as a member of the Council of Senior Scholars.

But al-Shithri was not alone in his hostility towards KAUST. Many of its advocates are afraid that if Abdullah is succeeded by a less reform-minded monarch, the university will quite simply be shut down. This would not be difficult, because the strictest security seals off the 36 square kilometre campus from the outside world. Although the university remains open for now, the results have been far from encouraging. Some of the facilities have after all been segregated as a result of pressure from conservative students—not the lecture halls, but the swimming pools and the students' dormitories. Even more important is that the student population remains small, amounting to 840 men and women in 2015,[9] by contrast with the 45,000 students at the Princess Nora University for women in Riyadh. The majority of this paltry total is foreign, as are the lecturers. Only 246 of the students are Saudis.

Even though the king endowed the university with the vast sum of 10 billion dollars, it has expanded very little. It continues to function but there is no sign at all that its example is being copied elsewhere in the country.

7

THE DIGITAL EXPLOSION

THE SOCIAL MEDIA—POWER AND THE DELUSION OF POWER

The statistics are clear as daylight—when it comes to social media, the Saudis are the leader on most platforms, especially on Twitter. Many young Saudis of both sexes go around with two or three smartphones in their pockets and are never offline. The penetration rate of mobile phones among Saudi nationals has climbed to 170 per cent, and 60 per cent of the population has an Internet connection. This percentage is growing daily. As for the group between eighteen and twenty-four years old, everyday Internet usage is huge (a good 90 per cent)—more than anywhere else in the Middle East. Saudi Arabia is no longer the closed society that it had been for so many years. Plenty of things can happen in cyberspace, even if there are limits.

Torrential downpours as a political issue

It was a long time before the monarchy permitted the use of the Internet, although this is hardly surprising if you recall that the introduction of radio and TV in the 1960s also led to commotion among the clergy. They were horrified when a woman's voice was first heard on the radio in 1963.

Two years later there was a violent attack on the first TV station in Riyadh. As for the Internet, the Saudis simply did not have access to it until the mid-1990s. In 1994 that changed, but only gradually. Initially only academic and medical bodies and research institutions were allowed to have broadband and it was only at the end of the millennium that the general public became linked up.

Since then things have proceeded at a headlong pace, faster than anywhere in the world. As for social media, there is no platform that is not made full use of in Saudi Arabia—Twitter, Facebook, YouTube, Blogger, Instagram, Plurk, Wikio, Flickr, Ning, Tumbler, Liriod, LinkedIn, Viber and WhatsApp. Twitter is expanding faster than the rest, with one out of three Saudis tweeting.[1] Saudi Arabia has the largest number of Twitter users relative to Internet users in the world.[2] Every month some 50 million tweets are sent (more than 1.5 million a day). What is more, it is only since March 2012 that Twitter has had an Arab-language interface. Facebook, which has had one since 2011, also does extremely well. It is growing faster in Saudi Arabia than anywhere else in the Gulf region and at the time of writing the country has about 8 million users out of a total population of approximately 30 million, giving it one of the highest percentages of Facebook users in the world.[3] YouTube is hardly less popular: Saudis view 90 million films a day; again, this is more than any other country in the world per head of the population.

As in other countries, by no means all the communication on social media is political in character; entertainment, religion and sport are the subjects that are mainly discussed, viewed or browsed. In the Gulf region at least, no research into this has yet been carried out. How can one account then for this eagerness to spend so many hours sitting and looking at a screen? One reason must be the absence of any offline entertainment—and in general the scarcity of public space. Saudi Arabia has no cinemas and hardly any theatres, while virtually everything can be accessed via the Internet. It is often said that YouTube enables you to see everything you want. Another explanation may be the great deal of leisure enjoyed by many Saudi citizens, and women in particular, due to high unemployment.

Admittedly there is a shortage of accurate data, but it remains probable that political issues are more often raised than before as a result of the use of social media. A good example is the political furore that breaks out every time Saudi Arabia is scourged by floods. Take Black Wednesday, 25 November 2009, when Jeddah and other parts of the Mecca region suffered downpours that led to colossal mudslides, turning the streets into rivers. It created havoc in the city, with at least 123 deaths, while some estimates were many times higher. The same day a Facebook group was formed, 'Popular Campaign to Save the City of Jeddah', and in a few days their pages had more than 40,000 followers. Those who 'liked' the campaign were indignant citizens who held the municipal authorities responsible for the abominable infrastructure—the city has no proper drainage system—and who called for heads to roll.[4] YouTube was inundated with films showing the scale of the disaster. Black Wednesday soon became a hot topic on various blogs and Internet forums. The governor of the region of Mecca, Prince Khaled bin Faisal Al Saud, was also not spared; nor were those who leapt to his defence, such as the well-known journalist, Jamal Khashoggi.

Four petitions then circulated on the Internet, each of them excoriating the local and regional authorities from its own perspective. The one that received the largest number of signatories was launched by a young lawyer, Waleed Abu al-Khair, who singled out corruption as one of the main reasons for the failure of the administration. 'Until recently our country was the kingdom of silence, but we are no longer going to let ourselves be intimidated,' he said in an interview at the time. (Later, half way through 2014, Abu al-Khair was detained—see below.) One of the other petitions, launched on the website of the human rights organisation ACPRA (Saudi Civil and Political Rights Association), which has since been dissolved by the courts, also called corruption an important cause, but went a step further by defining the catastrophe in Jeddah as 'genocide' and calling the 'princes of darkness' (notice the plural) to account. Floods have also occurred more recently.[5] Attention has been drawn to these events, especially by videos on YouTube, and emotional discussions were—and still are—held on Twitter. These torrential downpours have thus become a political theme.

An app for all occasions

In recent years, clerics, feminists and members of the royal family have also made use of social media. Despite their initial objections to the use of the mass media ('morally dangerous'), the clergy are presently among the most hands-on. This is especially the case with the 'non-official', non-establishment clergy who have succeeded in enlarging their sphere of influence enormously through Twitter, Facebook, YouTube and smartphone apps. The number of tweets from these quarters has grown by leaps and bounds since the uprisings in Tunisia and Egypt. The names one encounters most often are Muhammad al-Arefe, Aidh al-Qarnee and Salman al-Awda. Al-Arefe is the incontestable front-runner with at least 10.3 million followers; next comes al-Qarnee (the 'Dear Abby' of the Twitter sheikhs) with 7.7 million and al Awda with close to 6 million. Ahmed al-Shuqairi, the rock star—and self-appointed 'Elvis'—of the Saudi TV evangelists, deserves special mention. He is not a qualified cleric, but is no less popular for that—particularly because of his plea for a more relaxed form of Islam, as opposed to the prevailing rigid Wahhabi orthodoxy. Al-Shuqairi has 9 million followers on Twitter.[6]

Al-Awda proclaimed that religion and modern technology were not at odds, declaring on his Facebook page that 'Islam and Apple go hand in hand in close friendship and a brotherly relationship.' iTunes offers fans of al-Awda free apps with articles, sound clips, photos and links to his Twitter, Facebook and YouTube pages. The same app contains articles about him and there is also a direct link to his email address.[7] Muhammad al-Munajjid, another member of the clergy, who is also an active tweeter, is similarly Apple-minded—a free app comes with al-Munajjid's website 'Islam Question & Answer'.[8] It is available in eleven languages (including English, Arabic, Chinese, Russian, Spanish and French) and offers advice on a wide range of issues of Islamic doctrine, history and politics.

The views of these Internet preachers about the uprisings elsewhere in the Arab world or about political protest in Saudi Arabia itself vary greatly; some take the side of the authorities, others are savage in their criticism. The clerics who belong to the official religious establishment act largely as advocates for the regime, carrying out what 'the politicians' instruct them to do. Unlike many of his colleagues, however, the Grand Mufti Abd al-Aziz Al al-Sheikh is no enthusiastic supporter of the use of social media. He once announced that he regarded Twitter as a 'council of clowns' and 'dangerous for the faithful'. In October 2014 the grand mufti blasted the microblogging site as 'the repository of scourge and evil and the source of lies and falsehoods'.[9] However, he does share one thing with the other 'official' clergy, namely the belief that 'absolute obedience' (*wali al-amr*) is owed to the king. These and comparable statements regularly lead to emotional discussions in social and other media.

The clergy sometimes use the electronic media as a weapon, as was strikingly shown in the notorious case of Hamza Kashgari. At the beginning of 2012 this young Saudi launched a fictitious, critical debate with the Prophet Muhammad on Twitter. ('I do not like the halos of divinity around you. I shall not pray for you.') Twitter was inundated by a surge of angry Saudis, urged on by a number of old warhorses from the ranks of the ulama. In twenty-four hours there were 30,000 tweets, a large proportion of them calling for the death sentence, whether Kashgari repented or not. Blasphemy is a very serious offence—end of discussion. Kashgari had meanwhile fled to Malaysia, where he was soon arrested. He was extradited to Saudi Arabia and put in prison. An online petition calling for his release received 4,000 signatories, while his opponents, who called on Facebook for his immediate execution, soon ran up 21,000 'likes'. Following a two-year stint in jail, his first tweet read, 'Good morning to hope … to souls which never die … thank God.'

Digital feminism

It goes without saying that women make intensive use of modern means of communication as well. Slowly, but not necessarily surely, they are undermining the strict segregation that is so typical of Saudi society. Years ago girls and boys threw notes at each other with their phone numbers when they were standing on the escalator or passing each other in a shopping centre. This sort of clandestine activity is not necessary any longer; online forums, chatrooms, blogs, Facebook, SMS, Skype and Twitter offer abundant opportunities for contact. Despite all this online interaction, however, there is still a clear difference between the virtual and the real world, as is strikingly explained by a young woman student:

I had masses of friends of the other sex on the Internet, but it's still quite different if you meet each other in reality. … In Saudi Arabia if you're in the same space as someone of the opposite gender, it is almost the same as having intercourse. It's a shame, but that's how it is.

With regard to women's emancipation, the online actions of Saudi feminists, particularly those around the prohibition of driving, are what immediately come to mind. Some women get livid about the uninterrupted series of statements by leading preachers expressing hostility to their gender. The influential, blind cleric Abd al-Rahman al-Barrak, for instance, described women in the driving seat as being 'those who open the gates of evil'. In its turn, the Permanent Committee for Islamic Research and Issuing Fatwas, one of the highest religious bodies in the kingdom, reported that women driving cars would lead to 'a wave of prostitution, pornography, homosexuality and divorces', concluding delicately that within ten years 'there would be no more virgins'.[10] This sort of statement makes Saudi feminists furious, provoking them to actions that nobody would have dreamed of a decade ago and which reach far more people—virtually, at any rate.

The best-known example is Manal al-Sharif, the woman who posted a video of herself in the driving seat on YouTube and Facebook in May 2011 to the dismay of the authorities. It sparked off a passionate debate about the pros and cons of women driving via the hashtag #W2Drive. Her speech at the Oslo Freedom Forum in May 2012 has meanwhile been viewed almost 400,000 times on YouTube.[11] The price al-Sharif paid for her activism was the loss of her job as Internet security consultant at Saudi Aramco—a post she had held for ten years. After she refused to give up her activities, a leading Saudi cleric, Sheikh Abd al-Aziz al-Tarifi, issued a fatwa calling al-Sharif a 'munafiq', a religious hypocrite. After being fired and receiving many death threats, she left the country and took up residence abroad.

In the summer of 2012 a young Saudi woman gave an equally spectacular example of the use of social media on being ordered to leave the premises of a shopping centre by the religious police who were outraged at the sight of her varnished nails. She responded by arguing with them at the top of her voice while filming the event on her iPhone. The film was a hit on YouTube.[12]

The bitter squabble between the supporters and opponents of the segregation of the sexes continues unceasing. New incidents occur almost daily and they are encouraged or initiated more and more frequently by online campaigns. The Facebook petition at the beginning of 2011 which called for 'pure hospitals'—for women only, that is—caused another furore. The petition was largely applauded: 'Quite right too! Those doctors standing there between the legs of a girl should be stopped!' Someone else asked, 'Do you think it's all right for male doctors to look at your wife's genitals?' At one point the website Noor al-Yaqeen (Light of certainty) even called for segregation in the virtual world. The site forbids women from having contact with the clergy on its online forum, 'unless it is an emergency'. A senior cleric, Sheikh Abdullah al-Mutlaq, member of the Committee of Senior Scholars, warned that chatting between the sexes might indeed lead to sin. 'The devil would be present when women talk to men,' he specified.[13]

There are of course many online activists who express their disgust, such as Eman al-Nafjan, who speaks out openly for normal mingling of men and women on her Saudiwoman's Weblog, who is opposed to women being obliged to wear the niqab and who thinks women should be allowed to drive. It is striking, however, how many websites there are with female bloggers who actually defend the status quo and applaud the clerics.

The Julian Assange of Saudi Arabia

Members of the royal family are also increasingly visible in cyberspace, especially on Twitter. Until a few years ago Princess Ameerah, the wife of Prince al-Waleed bin Talal, led the way with 800,000 followers. For reasons that are not quite clear, her husband only started using Twitter in March 2013, but in the meantime he has acquired 2.6 million followers. At the end of 2011 the billionaire had invested $300 million in this new form of microblogging. Even some of the most high-ranking members of the royal family are on Twitter, including Crown Prince (now King) Salman bin Abd al-Aziz Al Saud, who acquired 200,000 followers in one fell swoop with his first tweet early in 2013; he now has more than a million.

If it is gossip one is looking for, especially of the scandalous variety, about members of the House of Saud, @mujtahidd ('The Diligent') is a spectacular source of information. With a little exaggeration he is sometimes called the 'Julian Assange of Saudi Arabia'.[14] Nobody knows precisely who he is—perhaps he is someone in the royal family who has been bypassed for rewards and honours. This Twitter user is generally well informed about spicy matters that normally remain secret. Although @mujtahidd fires his shots at a number of members of the royal family, his preferred target is Abd al-Aziz bin Fahd, the youngest son of the late King Fahd. This playboy and big spender gets his comeuppance with great regularity with the pretext that 'I am waging an aggressive battle against filthy corruption, a battle which begins by revealing who the corrupt are and which ends with their being fired.' He once asked the prince:

Is it true that your palace in Riyadh is bigger than that of the king and that it cost the state twelve billion riyals? Is it true that it stands on an estate of two million square metres and that it actually cost three billion to build, so that you've put away nine billion for yourself?

Sometimes his touch is more delicate: 'News has reached us that he [Abd al-Aziz bin Fahd] has postponed the jihad in Syria that he promised the sheikhs until he is back from his tour of nightclubs in New York and Paris.' Nothing and nobody is safe from his gall, not even the more progressive members of the royal family, such as the 'red prince', Talal bin Abd al-Aziz, and—it goes without saying—his plutocratic son, al-Waleed bin Talal. His mission is uncomplicated: 'It is not my task to tell people what they should do. It is my task to reveal the filthy truth; then people can decide for themselves what to do about it.' His following on Twitter continues to grow; in December 2014, it amounted to 1.62 million followers.

The limits of virtual protest

Do the authorities just let this all pass without comment? It is remarkable that Saudi Arabia does not instruct Internet providers to build in all kinds of censorship, although that could happen any day. Perhaps they turn a blind eye to so much freedom just because it gives them an excellent glimpse of what the population is talking about, while at the same time it serves as a safety valve for people's frustrations. It is striking that a group of angry young filmmakers has emerged who mainly make use of YouTube. A number of them have the status of media stars, such as the comedian

Omar Hussein with his successful programme *3al6ayer* (pronounced in Arabic as al-Tayer—'On the Fly'), which has been compared with Jon Stewart's *Daily Show*. The satirical show *La Yekthar* ('Keep a Lid on It'), by Fahad Albutairi, is equally popular with over 840,000 subscribers and over 80 million video views.[15] Many films are produced under the auspices of UTURN Entertainment, which has launched a whole series of YouTube celebrities and videos. In October 2013, for instance, Albutairi together with two other well-known comedians, Hisham Faqeeh and Alaa Wardi, produced the video 'No Woman No Drive', with a nod and a wink at Bob Marley. It had more than 3 million hits within two days of its posting. At the time of writing, this video has been viewed 12 million times. This satirical version of Marley's 1974 hit includes lines such as 'ovaries all safe and well, so you can make lots and lots of babies', which is a response to Sheikh Salah al-Luhaydan, a cleric who said women who drive risk damaging their ovaries and giving birth to children with defects. In a society like Saudi Arabia that is totally permeated with religion, humour and satire are bound to flourish. However that may be, it is a striking fact that these Saudi productions do well and not only in their own country—with its 2 million followers, *Eysh Elly* (What is) is the most viewed comedy in the Arab world.[16]

One last example is more of the educational variety. It is a YouTube clip which starts with the sentence 'Every year thousands of people are the victim of terrorism in Saudi Arabia; we are talking here of street terrorism!' The viewers are forcibly reminded of the fact that Saudi Arabia is number one in the world with regard to traffic deaths. The video has been viewed more than a million times and, what is even more surprising, the traffic police have started using it as information material.

There have always been limits of course, though it is only after the Arab Spring that the government started imposing more severe restrictions. It makes arbitrary use of regulations such as the one that states that 'it is forbidden to violate religious norms'. The anti-terror law of February 2014 provides prison and other punishments for vague offences such as 'harming the reputation of the kingdom' and 'sowing discord'. Citizens (among them excessively recalcitrant clerics such as Yusef al-Ahmed, professor at the Muhammad ibn Saud Islamic University), are frequently arrested and their Twitter and/or Facebook accounts get shut down. It is human rights activists, however, such as Abu al-Khair and Khaled al-Nasser, who are most often caught in the nets of this legislation. They are blatantly harassed by the Saudi authorities and every now and then their accounts get blocked—or worse. In July 2014, the Special Criminal Court in Jeddah sentenced Abu al-Khair to fifteen years imprisonment, followed by a fifteen-year travel ban. In 2009 he had established the website 'Human Rights Monitor'. He was found guilty of 'inciting public opinion', 'insulting the judiciary' and 'undermining the regime and officials'.[17]

Before the anti-terror law was put in place, others like Abdullah al-Hamid and Muhammad al-Qahtani were also paying a high price for their activities. Early in 2013 they were sentenced to eleven and ten years in prison respectively. Half way through 2013 seven activists from the Eastern Province were given sentences varying from five to ten years because they had 'incited people to protest' on Facebook. Raif Badawi, the founder of the 'Free Saudi Liberals' website, was sentenced to ten years in jail, 1,000 lashes and a fine. The old warhorse Sheikh Abd al-Rahman al-Barrak added insult to injury by issuing a fatwa in which he labelled Badawi an 'unbeliever … and apostate who must be tried and sentenced according to what his words require'.[18]

It is not uncommon for websites to be blocked—in February 2014, for example, forty-one news sites were closed down—and sometimes whole Internet services are even taken off the air. This happened to the Internet phone and texting programme Viber in June 2013 to the frustration of 10 million users. The response of Twitter user @jabertoon was to the point, 'The worst thing about Viber being blocked is not the blocking itself, but the fact that it treats people like a bunch of children.' The Communications and Information Technology Commission (CITC) is planning to attack Skype and WhatsApp. Even more alarming was the news circulated on Twitter that the authorities were to review the Anti-Cybercrime Law so as to initiate legal proceedings against networking sites such as Twitter for allowing accounts which 'promote adultery, homosexuality and atheism'.[19] The relative freedom of Saudi YouTubers is also under attack as they will soon be required to get registered and obtain a licence to be able to carry on with their activities.[20] Half way through 2014 *The Economist* reported that in the Eastern Province, where the population is mainly Shiite, cell-phone users discovered to their horror that they had unintentionally down-loaded spyware. The government uses software, described as a 'remote control device' (RCS), to gain access to all users' information.[21]

Since the new anti-terrorism law has come into force the authorities have clearly increased their control of the social media. As Kristin Diwan rightly observed: 'Its sweeping definition of terrorism as any act that desta-bilizes public order or harms national unity would seem to cover just about any type of dissent.'[22] Not surprisingly, Saudis soon started criticising the new law, under the crypto-ironic hashtag 'In Mozambique'.

The fact that the Saudi authorities are not the only ones capable of con-trolling what takes place on the Internet was demonstrated in May 2013 when the hackers' collective, Anonymous, succeeded in blocking a number of government sites, including those of the ministries of finance and foreign affairs. Via the Twitter campaign @OpSaudi, the hackers were protesting against the government's plans to deploy Mobily, the largest telecom com-pany in the country, to supervise Internet communications. When Mobily denied that this was the case, the hackers reacted with an action that was as predictable as it was radical and Mobily's own website was shut down. A few months later, the same collective launched a cyber-attack on both the Syrian and the Saudi Arabian governments to punish both sides in the Syrian civil war for their atrocities. The hackers' collective accused the Saudi government of backing rebel fighters linked to al-Qaeda.

The absence of any tradition of street protest

Are the social media a force for revolution? While there is a considerable group of 'cyber optimists', increasing numbers of people are casting a criti-cal eye on what they call technological fetishism ('the more social media, the better'). As the godfather of 'cyber realism', Evgeny Morozov, never tires of explaining, it is not the Internet that makes people free, it is the people themselves that do that.[23] Internet can be an aid, but that is all it is, and it can just as easily be used by regimes in power and they sometimes deploy it even more adroitly than the opposition. It is not just a question of the many possibilities of exerting control that a regime has at its disposal, but also of the use of Internet by government officials, either on their own initiative or by way of confidants, paid or otherwise. They do their best to guide discussions in a specific direction. Sometimes that works; on other occasions, it does not—Saudi Arabia is no exception to this rule. In opposition circles, tweeting civil servants can be spotted a mile off—they are mockingly labelled 'egg heads', after the oval-shaped empty space where their profile photo ought to be.

As in other countries, in Saudi Arabia the underlying social and political dynamics are more important than the technology, whether the forms are new or not. It is this dynamic that decides whether an opposition movement has a chance of surviving or not. At best social media can serve to speed up a process of this sort. In the Saudi context this has been made painfully clear on various occasions—during the Day of Rage on 11 March 2011 and during the women's protest movement launched in mid-2011 by Manal al-Sharif. After al-Sharif's arrest a Facebook page was started calling for a national protest (under the name 'Women2Drive'). The page received 10,000 'likes' in next to no time, but to many people's consternation only a few dozen women actually went and sat in the driving seat. Something similar occurred with the Facebook page early in 2011 that called for a general nationwide protest, inspired by the mass demonstrations in Tunisia and Egypt. The fact that an anonymous Facebook page should provoke a government response in the form of a huge police presence, with helicopters flying overhead, does of course say something about the power of social media. Just as important, however, was the fact that on the day itself, 11 March 2011, only one demonstrator showed up; some Saudis even started cynically referring to the Day of Rage as the Day of Calm.

Saudi Arabia has had no experience of the phenomenon of modern collective action such as emerged elsewhere in the Arab and Islamic world. The 'street' has never been the theatre of protest, with the marked exception of the Eastern Province where street protest has become an inseparable part of the unrest of the Shiite part of the population (see Chapter 9, 'Curse the Shiites!'). An important factor is that the economic situation is nowhere near as wretched as, say, in Egypt. A political scientist at the King Saud University has his own ideas on the matter. 'Maybe people are more rational than we tend to assume. They calculate before they go on to the street as their Arab brothers did elsewhere. They look around. And what do they see?'

For now there seems to be considerable support for the new king and hostility towards even the suggestion of demonstrations. For every activist blogger who is arrested or whose life is destroyed, there are ten tribal Internet discussion forums where people can beat their breasts proclaiming their loyalty to the king and the Saudi monarchy. Some of these forums have between 50,000 and 100,000 users. When all is said and done, a genuine Day of Rage may have to wait a while.

8

THE TASK OF ART

A MISSION FOR CHANGE

Jeddah has always been different, more liberal and not averse to experiment. It is a port city through which pilgrims and merchants from all quarters have passed over the centuries, by contrast with Riyadh in the barely accessible interior of the peninsula, which is conservative and rejects the new.

It says a great deal about change in Saudi Arabia then that even in Riyadh a couple of art galleries have opened. In Jeddah, of course, anything can happen. You may even come across a local pop group having a jam session. There are some who label the people of Jeddah apostates, not real Muslims. Yiding Cao, who is originally from China and worked as the manager of Alāan Artspace in Riyadh when we visited in 2013, obviously has another take on this and says admiringly, 'Jeddah is different. That's where it all happens!'

The Wahhabi form of Islam that prevails in Saudi Arabia is opposed to art on principle. Traditional Islamic calligraphy is acceptable, but in this strictest interpretation of Islam the depiction of people or animals is regarded as taboo, as it can all too easily lead to idolatry.

The only museums in Saudi Arabia are historical ones, but some galleries have recently opened, including in Riyadh. This is something that is happening more often in the kingdom; in theory it is not permitted, and yet it still happens, as long as there is not too much objection from conservative quarters. Art education remains a step too far, however, with the result that the population at large either lacks any rudimentary information about it or else shows no serious interest in the subject. According to Yiding of Alāan Artspace, this is why the founders of the gallery have latched on to something that does exist—namely a passion for food. If you want an evening out in Saudi Arabia, you go out to dinner. Alāan Artspace consists of a café, a restaurant and an exhibition space. 'Eat and art,' says Yiding. Alāan Artspace opened in October 2012 with the exhibition 'Soft Power', consisting solely of work by women artists. In view of Saudi reality, this was 'extremely challenging', says Yiding. Visitors were particularly struck by a video of a wrecked car being retrieved from the demolition dump and painted pink. The unstated theme of the work was the prohibition of women driving. Another object was *Esmee* (My name), an installation of beads in which women had etched their names. Anyone who looks twice at this work will see it as an attack on the tradition that required women to behave like anonymous black phantoms.

Alāan means 'now'. The gallery is devoted to contemporary art that provokes people to think about the state of things today. It does not aim to offend:

We want to touch lightly on things in everyday life, so that people start to ask themselves why something is as it is. That's what we're here for. We hope that visitors will go and sit around the table to browse in the art books we have made available. There are also workshops—all this is intended to compensate for the fact that there is no art education.

Half a year after it opened, Alāan Artspace had attracted around 1,000 visitors. They hear of the gallery by word of mouth—people are enthusiastic and tell others about it—and via social media. The café at the front of the premises is replaced from time to time by a commercial pop-up shop with popular design articles, in the expectation that young customers will proceed from there to the exhibition space.

THE TASK OF ART

Pushing the limits

All the works by Alāan's stable of artists that hang or are planned to hang in the gallery have to be screened by the Ministry of Culture and Information. Yet there are portraits hanging here, despite the fact that figurative art is haram. This is a very sensitive area, however. 'Full frontal is not possible, certainly when there's a woman depicted. But the artists take advantage of what's possible, by using a certain angle of light or making a face blurred. We don't break the rules, but we do try to push the limits.'

You often hear young people saying this sort of thing—that they do not want to offend people or provoke a confrontation, but rather to teach people to dream about progress. 'I sometimes think that if you provoke people, or put too much pressure on them, you don't get your message across,' says Haifaa al-Mansour.

Mansour is a unique case, a young female filmmaker in a country where women take the back seat and where there are no cinemas (although there are apparently serious plans to start building them sometime in 2015). She has succeeded in making a feature film in Saudi Arabia that has received awards in various film festivals abroad and which has even been submitted by the Saudi authorities for an Oscar, albeit unsuccessfully. Her film, *Wadjda*, is about a girl who has set her heart on getting a bike. And she does not give up, even though everyone tells her that girls do not ride bikes.

'We are living in exciting times now in Saudi Arabia,' says Mansour. 'I think that things are going to become more open. We have to be realistic though; change doesn't come overnight. If you go to the big, glossy shopping centres in Riyadh and the other major cities you may get a misleading impression. They conceal how conservative people are under the surface. There are a great many conservatives who think that woman shouldn't be allowed to make a film, because that is a threat to Islamic values as they see them. And who think that women shouldn't assert themselves in this way in public. When I wrote the script I made an effort to be careful when I was dealing with sensitive subjects. I wanted to make a film that gives people hope.'

The Saudi authorities respond in just as an illogical or perhaps pragmatic way to cinemas and films as they do to art and galleries. In mid-November 2014, *Arab News* reported that relevant government bodies, including the mutawwa, had given the green light to the establishment of cinema houses.[1] But no cinemas immediately materialised. Thus far they are banned, because even if you segregate the audience, a warm dark room like a cinema is bound to lead to immorality and other ungodly horrors. A lot of Saudis go to the cinema in neighbouring Bahrain. Films do get seen—after all, it is hardly possible to prohibit satellite TV, videos and DVDs. In neighbouring Iran, the authorities have been trying to block them for years, yet all the most recent films are still available and satellite dishes are only occasionally removed as a token reminder that they are forbidden. Haifaa Mansour's film is simply shown on Saudi TV.

As a woman in a country without any cinemas, how do you come by the idea of making a film?

It's just love of film. I don't try to make a political statement or to be heroic. I grew up in a very small town in a family with twelve children; I'm number eight. There wasn't much to do there, so we watched a huge number of films at home. It was a very small world and films gave me my chance to see the world. Those were the happiest hours of my childhood.

She felt that her services were not valued by the oil company where she worked:

A great many young women are not taken seriously. I wanted to do something that would make me happy, so I produced a short film, just for myself. I took it to a film festival in Abu Dhabi, and people there were totally amazed! My goodness, a film director, who is not only Saudi but a woman as well! I wear this label with pride. I hope I'll be able to inspire lots of young women to make films.

Support from the family

In Saudi Arabia a woman can make a career as an artist or in the business world and in many other fields. The absolute precondition is that one has the support of one's family, and in particular the male members—one's father, brother or husband. And so far there has been little or no change in this. The change that has occurred is that more and more families support their daughters if they want to pursue a career:

My father always said—you can succeed if you really want something. The only thing is that you have to work hard. I come from an ordinary family, not a rich one or one where we were educated abroad. My parents attached a great deal of value to education. But it's really important to have the support of the man who controls your life, your guardian, that is.

On top of that, of course, it is easier for a woman to make a career in education or the health sector than in art. Art remains a sensitive issue for the still sizeable conservative segment of the population and the clerics. Making films is a challenge. If you shoot on location you have to take the people who live there into account:

For instance, I couldn't film the outdoor street scenes myself if I didn't want a confrontation. People don't expect to see a woman in the middle of the street giving directions and working with men. I respected that and followed my actors indoors on a screen, using a walkie-talkie to direct them. I work in the system, whether that is an explicit requirement or not.

In the end this has made me a better director. Every obstacle has a hidden positive aspect. The situation in the Middle East and Saudi Arabia is extremely difficult, but if all you do is complain about what doesn't work, nothing will work for you. You do better to find out what does work. There's plenty of change. Even five years ago it was impossible to make films in Saudi Arabia.

So much more is possible in Jeddah than in Riyadh. There has been a modest film festival there for years. And yet it was there, of all places, that the festival was suddenly banned. Does that not mean that all change can be wiped out at the drop of a hat?

There are plenty of Saudis who are afraid of this. They are wrong, says Mansour. She does not think so:

There is a great deal of art currently, there are also a lot of writers and my film is made in Saudi Arabia. That's a better indicator than what happened in Jeddah. Just remember, children have Internet, they go abroad and if anything they want to benefit even more from life, rather than go back to a protected environment where they can't do anything. Many of the changes can't be seen from the outside, but there's plenty going on beneath the surface.

Saudi Art Guide

It is certainly true that plenty of things have changed, but even in liberal Jeddah artists have to watch their step. Take the graphic designer Soraya

Darwish, one of the driving spirits behind the Saudi Art Guide.[2] 'In a nutshell, it's the first online guide to cultural events and galleries in Saudi Arabia. You always heard by chance if something was going on; people thought there wasn't any art scene here, so our idea was to do something about that.'

If you ask Darwish about sensitivities in society and censorship and how artists steer a course around it, she refers you to her article on the blog Hyperallergic, titled 'What Is and Isn't Art in Saudi Arabia?'.[3] 'That should answer your question', she says. 'Here in Jeddah I have to be diplomatic.' For Western readers she is too cautious, even in the article, to tell them anything new.

The issue of art education, or rather the lack of it, is debated in the article among other subjects. Censorship forms an obstacle for everyone who advocates art being on the curriculum as it should be:

The parents of a student at a famous private school lodged a complaint against a teacher who let the pupils see images of nudes. A huge number of works in art history show nudity; yet schools and universities refuse to include them in their curricula. It is time to take matters into our own hands.

And this is what people are doing, and not just through the art books on the table in Alāan Artspace. Take the Amen Art Foundation run by the conceptual artist Abdulnasser Gharem. Gharem is one of the most famous contemporary artists of Saudi Arabia—perhaps the most famous. The Amen Art Foundation is his most recent project; it aspires to create the best environment for artists in Riyadh, one of the most conservative cities in Saudi Arabia with a reputation for being hard and unyielding. 'You can't buy an expensive camera here, or find a studio or even come across an art book,' says Gharem. The Amen Foundation will fulfil those functions; it will be a library, a studio and a darkroom, and Abdulnasser Gharem will be on the spot to assist the artists.

Gharem is a painter who came to the conclusion in 2003 that he had more to tell in his paintings and could get a bigger public if he went out on to the street. So he did just that, with a group of people, and painted the surface of a collapsed bridge near his native town with the word *siraat* (the path). Speaking in Riyadh, he says, 'For a Muslim the word "path" is very highly charged. You utter it more than a hundred times a day when you pray. Being a Muslim has to do with following the right path.'

Siraat has become the work on which he has based his fame, and videos of it have been bought by various international museums. It was a performance, but it was also a new path. It literally means the beginning of the era of contemporary art in Saudi Arabia:

People here are also looking for a new path. I was trying to find a common cause that could bring us together to think about our ideas or to decide where we need to look. The far end of the bridge has been demolished. It is an end, but an open one.

Thinking for oneself

Gharem is also a good example of a prominent Saudi who aims to achieve change without provoking either the civil authorities or the clergy. 'I don't want any conflict,' he says. 'I want to find a new angle of approach for looking at something and then presenting it to people.' His aim is to get people thinking for themselves.

'They are trying to murder art,' according to a Saudi intellectual, who wishes to remain anonymous. But with 'they', she was not referring just to the ultra-conservative clergy. King Abdullah had created a little space, but all too often it is the civil servants, or public officials responsible for implementing policy, who put their foot on the brake, fearful of conservative opposition. In Gharem's view, however, it is also the people themselves who stand in the way of change.

The educational system spreads ignorance, he adds. If you go to the library, you see what he is talking about. 'There are only Islamic books there; you can't find any book about art or music. When you ask a question, all you get for an answer is a thousand-year old proverb. They don't allow you to think for yourself in the age in which you are living.'

Among Gharem's most famous works are roadblocks and traffic signs:

I put them in front of people, so that they don't know what they are supposed to do. Society creates these 'roadblocks'; it can't move. The barriers I make are covered with stamps containing the text, 'Don't trust concrete.' We put a block in front of ourselves with some stupid idea or other from some viewpoint or other, without analysing it. That's what I am against. That's my mission.

Gharem is one of the most important pioneers of conceptual art in Saudi Arabia. The confusing thing is that he is also a soldier, a lieutenant colonel in the army—'in about six months' time I'll be promoted to the rank of brigadier general'. How can you be a good soldier and a good artist at the same time—the notion of being obedient to orders versus that of spiritual and intellectual freedom?

I come from a small town in the south. In those days, more than twenty years ago, it meant something if you became an officer. Nobody was interested in my special talent. The family thought it was a disaster—it is haram, taboo; what are you going to do? I was frustrated in my mission to become an artist. But the army gave me the power to be patient with my mission.

In its turn the army does not want to lose him:

I'm good in technology, so I develop all kinds of things for them. And the army is fond of me now; recently they've started making allowances for my work as an artist and they've given me three years furlough. That is the power of art. The soldiers see how useful I am for the country.

The artist's task, according to Gharem, is to create a link between result and motive:

To confront society with the question—why is this the way it is? What are people hiding, what are our underlying motives? And to find a common language which everyone understands, so they can become involved. Art must be a platform that everyone can approach, where they can think about themselves and talk about their habits and their reference points. Is something oppressive? Does it work properly? I enjoy sparking off this sort of brainstorming. But it's the people themselves who have to bring about changes, not the artist—that is not his task.

At an auction of Christie's in Dubai in 2011, Gharem's work *Message/Messenger* was bought for over $800,000 by a collector—a staggering sum for a Saudi artist. He put all the money into the Amen Art Foundation. Why 'Amen'?

You find the word 'Amen' in all religions; it is a peaceful word, you can settle an angry exchange with it. In my childhood I suffered because I couldn't find any books, nor could I meet any other artists to advise me. Now I have the knowledge and the credibility to help others. And I learned from the army that you are responsible for your people, that you have a mission and that you have to succeed. I'll go crazy in Riyadh, but that won't stop me.

Is there in fact much interest among the younger generation for art?

I work on YouTube with young people. Every film they make gets five million viewers. Stand-up comedy—that sort of thing. They sit, about six of them in a little office, and reach two hundred million viewers a year. They do it on YouTube because the official channels would never accept what they do. But they get a bigger public than they would ever have had in a theatre.

I can see the change already. Nobody knows exactly what is going on, but there is some movement. The king took a terrific initiative in setting up scholarships for young people to get an education abroad. We now have some 200,000 young Saudis in different countries. After three years they come back and are enormously changed. That's why I also work on my foundation, so that when they get back home, they'll have a platform and can keep on doing what they've been doing. Photography, short films, all sorts of things.

The battle is not yet over; these pioneers, Gharem, Mansour and other artists, also face a lot of opposition. 'Of course I get hostile reactions,' Mansour says nonchalantly. Hate mail, she means. 'But that's okay, I don't take it personally. Everyone gets it, sometimes. We're not fighting a war.'
Gharem also takes no notice:

There's a saying that goes, if nobody hates you, you must be doing something wrong. In the end, it's about my mission, and it makes no difference to me. I know what I have to do; after these big projects I'm going to expand my organisation. I want to set the artists and the galleries a good example, to encourage others. Abdulnasser says it: yes we can! I'm not like the others who complain. I don't just say I'll set up a foundation, I do it straightaway. I'm now going to Berlin and Venice, to collect people's ideas everywhere, to find out what is the best approach. The people here need an example.

9

'CURSE THE SHIITES!'

THE FORGOTTEN REVOLT
OF A MARGINALISED MINORITY

Are Shiites really Muslims? According to some Saudis they are not. They think that Shiites spit in their food, for instance, so that it is difficult for Sunnis and Shiites to eat together. Or that it is unclean to shake hands with a Shiite, making a ritual ablution necessary. All too often, however, Shiites are denoted as *rawafid* (those who reject the 'true Islam') whose loyalty lies with Iran rather than with Saudi Arabia. This notion is not only held by religious literalists but is widespread among the Saudi population—even among the most educated and cosmopolitan Saudis. Shiites in turn feel that they are the subject of discrimination and do everything they can to put an end to it, including holding mass demonstrations. What are the roots of this protest and what forms has it taken since the Arab Spring? Maybe the most important question is whether the Shiites are in a position to make effective overtures towards the Sunni opposition.

Second-class citizens

Discrimination against the Shiite minority, which amounts to about 10 to 15 per cent of the population, the majority of whom live in the Eastern

Province with its abundant resources of oil, goes back to the time of Ibn Saud.[1] In 1913 he conquered the oases of al-Ahsa and Qatif where the majority of the inhabitants were Shiites and they have been treated as second-class citizens ever since their formal incorporation into the Kingdom of Saudi Arabia (1932). Shiites have almost no say in the local or provincial councils, nor do they hold any senior posts in sensitive ministries such as the Ministry of Interior or the Ministry of Defence or in the National Guard. They are also excluded from offices at the court or in the cabinet.

Even if the government has taken measures to rid school textbooks of anti-Shiite rhetoric, teachers frequently depict Shiites as 'infidels'. By now it is normal for boys' schools in the Eastern Province to have a Shiite head, but this is not the case with girls' schools. Religious studies lessons are taught by Sunni teachers in every school. There is nowhere for parents or pupils to turn to if they want to complain about matters like this. Hamza, a self-assured Shiite secondary school pupil, says that it is almost impossible to take such complaints to the courts: 'Who am I supposed to appeal to? A judge who is a Wahhabi sheikh?'

Hussein al-Alak, a human rights activist in his early thirties, is typical of the widely felt dissatisfaction. 'It is really depressing,' he says. 'I don't see any solution unless drastic changes take place.' He visited the United States once and remarked that 'There are a strikingly large number of parallels between the situation of Afro-Americans in the period before the civil rights movement and the Saudi Shiites today. When I talked to black Americans about it, I had the feeling I was talking to Shiites.' Tawfiq al-Saif, a prominent Shiite intellectual, is every bit as outspoken. 'Some demands simply can't be postponed. Of course I know that not all Sunnis are treated equally, but we are humiliated systematically!'

The living standard among Shiites has admittedly improved over the years, but the sense of being discriminated against remains unabated. A good example is Awamiyya, in the Eastern Province. It is an impoverished little town, even though a huge gas pipeline runs past it, which the residents receive no benefit from at all. An appallingly high percentage of the population is unemployed, and the walls of the city are covered with slogans like 'Death to the Wahhabis', 'Down with the government' and 'We will never forget our prisoners'. During a meeting of young Shiites in the neighbouring town of Safwa, one of them commented, 'We get high from the situation; we don't need alcohol or drugs!'

The sense of political and social and economic exclusion is further aggravated by religious discrimination. The puritanical Wahhabi variety of Sunni Islam decides everything, and Shiites simply do not count. In the highest religious body, the Council of Senior Scholars, they are also not represented. At a local level discrimination takes the form of a lack of mosques of its own denomination or other religious facilities such as *huseiniyyas* (community spaces where services can also be held). In the central square of Qatif the government has built a large Sunni mosque, while at the same time it is almost impossible for Shiites to get permission to build a mosque in towns or villages where they do not form a majority. Saudi Shiites are forbidden from holding their annual traditional procession for the holy day of Ashura, except in Qatif. On this day, Shiites commemorate the martyrdom of Imam Hussein at the Battle of Karbala in 680.

Cosmetic reforms

The notion prevails among Saudi Sunnis that it is impossible by definition for Shiites to be loyal to the state. What they have in mind is above all the institution of the *marja al-taqlid* (source of emulation): every Shiite is obliged to choose a higher religious leader and to obey his instructions in spiritual, legal and sometimes even political domains. Even though the vast majority of the Shiites in the Eastern Province do not follow Iran's Supreme Leader Ayatollah Ali Khamenei as their *marja*, most Saudis assume that they do. Shiite leaders never tire of explaining that their loyalty to the Saudi state has never been in doubt. According to the above-mentioned Tawfiq al-Saif, 'There is not a shred of evidence that Saudi Shiites are loyal to anyone other than the Saudi state and this has been the case since the kingdom was founded.' It is an extremely sensitive issue and a recurring topic in numerous conversations.

The assumptions of the Sunnis are not entirely without foundation, however. In 1979 the Saudi Shiites initially drew a great deal of inspiration from the Iranian Islamic revolution. In that year also the spiritual leader Hassan al-Saffar and some others founded the 'Islamic Revolution Organisation in the Arabian Peninsula' (the IRO). Tens of thousands of people held regular demonstrations in the streets of Qatif at the end of 1979 and early 1980—protests that usually ended in skirmishes with the National Guard, resulting in dozens of deaths.

The leaders of the IRO were sent into exile, but in 1993 they returned after coming to an agreement with the government. In exchange for a general amnesty they agreed to cease making anti-Saudi propaganda. After a short-lived interruption to their activities, Shiites under the leadership of al-Saffar channelled their activities through a movement which is known as the Islahiyyin (Reformists). They distanced themselves more emphatically than they had done before both from violence and from Iran and the Iranian model, in which politics and religion are so intertwined that the supreme spiritual leader also holds the highest political post.

Most of the supporters of the Reformists chose Grand Ayatollah Ali al-Sistani as their 'source of emulation'. He was admittedly born in Iran but has for many years been the most important Shiite religious leader in Iraq. More important still, he is their favourite *marja* because he is an outspoken advocate of a separation of religion and politics. Some of his supporters even described him as a *marja ilmani*, or secular *marja*. In an interview, in his office in Qatif, the spiritual leader al-Saffar used subtle terminology, 'We are not talking about a religious state or about a secular system by definition. What we want is a "civil state" [*dawla madaniyya*], with equal rights for everyone.'

After a period of relative calm, the tension between the Shiites and Sunnis came to the surface once again in 2003. The Iraq war, which resulted in a Shiite-dominated government in Baghdad, was the most important provocation. The Saudi government saw this as an 'Iranian take-over' of Iraq and it formed a pretext for sectarianism to become rife in the country once again. Crown Prince Abdullah did his best to pour oil on the troubled waters, for instance by launching a National Dialogue, to which Shiites were also invited, and also by holding local government elections, but his activities stalled at the level of well-meaning proposals. The former chairman of the municipal council of Qatif, the activist Jafar al-Shayeb, made no attempt to disguise his disappointment: 'It still remains at the level of a talking-shop. There are no instruments to convert recommendations into concrete, practical projects.' A series of much-discussed 'reforms' turned out to be mainly cosmetic, even after Abdullah's ascent to the throne in 2005. The only ray of hope was King Abdullah's project for scholarships abroad which Shiite students could benefit from as well, without discrimination.

In the years that followed there was yet more unrest. In February 2009 major disturbances took place in Medina when Shiite pilgrims attempted to visit the tombs of their imams. Prince Nayef bin Abd al-Aziz Al Saud, the ultra-conservative minister of interior, who had held government office since 1975, defended the brutal conduct of the religious police with the statement that Saudi Arabia 'follows the doctrine of Sunni Islam [and although some citizens] conform to other schools of Islam, they will be well advised to respect this doctrine'.[2] The response was demonstrations in the Eastern Province, the largest since the events of 1979–80, which were put down with disproportionate violence.

The series of violent confrontations exacerbated the differences within the Shiite community about the speed and nature of the reforms. There was a growing gap between the Islahiyyin (or 'notables'), who still hoped to obtain concessions through dialogue with the government and another more radical group. The latter were inspired by Hamza al-Hassan, who was living in exile in London, but the consistently outspoken Sheikh Nimr al-Nimr was an even greater influence. While the influence of the latter was initially confined to his hometown of Awamiyya, it gradually extended far beyond it. In March 2009 he denounced the minister of interior yet again for his discriminatory policies, drawing a conclusion that was as unexpected as it was radical, namely that, if the discrimination did not stop, the only option left was secession. His statement provoked great discomfort not only in the ranks of the Shiite notables but also in the government. The sheikh and a number of his younger followers were promptly arrested, which led straightaway to an exponential increase in al-Nimr's popularity. The gap between the older and the younger generation became ever greater after 2009, as demonstrated by incidents inspired by the uprisings in Tunisia and Egypt.

The fat is in the fire

The initial response came mainly from the older group of Shiite activists. Encouraged by the downfall of presidents Ben Ali and Mubarak, they drew up the Declaration of National Reform, with signatories from a wide range of Saudi citizens, representing a variety of ideologies and sectarian persuasions. This petition and some other ones launched at the same time won no concessions either from the provincial or the national authorities. The younger activists therefore concluded that the time for the 'soft' forms of action of the old guard was over and called for demonstrations. Although the slogans used were moderate—'We don't want any regime change' and 'Neither Sunni, nor Shia, but Islamic unity'—every demonstration ended with dozens of arrests and many injuries. The fury of the demonstrators was directed above all at the governor of the Eastern Province, Prince Muhammad bin Fahd, notorious for his draconian measures against his Shiite opponents.

At the same time, a major three-day conference was held in Riyadh entitled 'The Truth about Shia Islam and the Danger it Poses for the Sunni'. And if this title was not clear enough, the names given to some of the panel discussions allowed for no ambiguity: 'Shiite Crimes Throughout History' and 'The Worldwide Shiite Project'. Shiite leaders were convinced that this conference of prominent Wahhabi clerics and academics had the full blessing of the government and they responded as such. 'The government is mobilising public opinion against the Shiites. It creates a foundation for discrimination against us and is extremely dangerous,' said Sadek al-Ramadan, the director of the Qatif-based Adala Centre for Human Rights.

The fat was really in the fire after Saudi troops were sent to Bahrain on 14 March 2011 to support the efforts of the Bahraini monarchy in crushing the Shiite rebellion there. In Riyadh they were convinced that Bahrain should be prevented at all costs from becoming a 'Shiite Cuba'. In the days that followed, thousands of Shiites demonstrated in most of the towns and villages of the Eastern Province in solidarity with their co-religionists. The Saudi regime was quick to respond with both sectarian propaganda and further repression.

Similar to the prelude to the Day of Rage, prominent clerics again issued fatwas declaring that the demonstrations were 'illegal' and would lead to *fitna* (chaos). Young demonstrators wondered why they were not permitted to demonstrate. 'Our government supports the revolutionaries in Syria, how can they ban us from going out on to the streets?' said twenty-year-old

Ahmed. Just as before, sectarian sentiments were stirred up by social media and on YouTube in particular. In addition the regime resorted to a whole armoury of repressive measures to crush the protests. Not only was new, strict legislation for online newspapers introduced; censorship was also imposed on YouTube and Facebook and many websites were blocked.

In the autumn of 2011 matters got totally out of hand. While the Shiite leaders were discussing matters with the government, more than 200 demonstrators were arrested, including the popular cleric Tawfiq al-Amir, and a virtually permanent state of siege was imposed on Qatif with the authorities deploying helicopters, armoured vehicles and a large police force. The first deaths occurred at the beginning of November, with five people killed by the police. The Ministry of Interior had meanwhile poured oil on the flames by again talking about 'foreign elements', as if to imply that the demonstrators were agents of Iran. They were expected to state clearly 'whether their loyalty lay with God and their native country or with that state [Iran] and its authority'.[3] Prince Nayef added that he would crush the protests with an 'iron hand'. Early in 2012 his ministry published a list of twenty-three 'most wanted' troublemakers, the same tactics as had previously been employed for al-Qaeda terrorists. Mansour al-Turki, the ministry spokesman, announced in no uncertain terms that the people on the list formed part of a criminal organisation with a 'foreign agenda'.

The demonstrations continued almost uninterrupted, with the situation becoming ever grimmer, as was reflected in the slogans the protesters used, such as 'Death to the House of Saud'. Sheikh Nimr al-Nimr, provocative as always, delivered a sermon in February 2012 in which he called for the abolition of the monarchy. When demonstrators threw an effigy of Prince Nayef in front of the wheels of an armoured car, live ammunition was fired once more. By the end of 2012 more than sixteen protesters had died, most of them from Awamiyya.

Young and old

In recent years young activists in the Eastern Province have become increasingly impatient and the older generation has lost much of its authority as a result. Many of the younger generation take the view that the Islahiyyin have allowed themselves to be 'taken for a ride' by the royal family and have been given nothing in return. Things have to be done differently and faster, they argue. 'Nobody in the younger generation trusts the government. … It is high time to change it,' says a nineteen-year-old student in Qatif. Tawfiq al-Saif, himself one of the first generation of activists, acknowledges this phenomenon: 'The younger generation is telling the leaders to stop. You haven't achieved anything. It's our turn now.' One of his colleagues, Jafar al-Shayeb, expresses himself in similar terms, while also adding that increased radicalisation is on the cards. 'The youth want to see quick results and we will do our best to make the government aware of this. We are trying to keep control of the situation, but at a certain moment that will no longer be possible.'

These older activists are aware that they get very few results by continuing to talk with the government, but they also wonder what the alternatives are. 'Do the demonstrators have a programme? And does Sheikh Nimr al-Nimr really believe in democracy?' are other issues raised in these circles. Sometimes they also criticise the naivety of the young who think they can launch a movement in Saudi Arabia on the model of Cairo's Tahrir Square. 'We are a minority; we are just a province; we can't carry out any revolution,' one of them remarks cautiously.

The popularity of Sheikh al-Nimr, who is distrusted by some older activists, remains undiminished among the young. He is admired for saying things that other people think but do not dare to say. When the much-feared minister of interior died in June 2012, it was reason for al-Nimr to 'rejoice over his death' and to hope that 'he will be eaten by the worms and that the terrors of hell will await him'. In the same breath, he prayed to God to 'carry off the dynasties of Saud, Khalifa [Bahrain] and Assad'.[4] That was clearly going too far and he was arrested once more, after some skirmishes in which he was shot in the leg. His arrest gave rise to new protests and renewed violence, including by some of the demonstrators who threw Molotov cocktails at police patrols and government buildings. Activists circulated calls on the Internet to 'attack police stations and blow up oil wells' if al-Nimr was not released. Once more the police used live ammunition with deadly results and the government continued with its relentless pursuit of the 'list of twenty-three'.

Once again the older activists were caught in a dilemma of whether to choose the side of the revolutionary youth or to continue to maintain a dialogue with the government. In an attempt to pour water on the flames, Shiite clerics issued two statements condemning all use of violence. One of the statements spoke positively about King Abdullah's intention to set up a 'centre for dialogue' in Riyadh. The revolutionary youth thought this proposal was far too half-hearted and friendly to the regime. One of them remarked cynically, 'This statement is just saying the same thing as the government—"Stop the protests, you are creating *fitna*."'[5]

Unbridgeable gap

Between the summer of 2012 and early 2013 protests also took place elsewhere in the country, both in the province of al-Qassim—the conservative heartlands of Saudi Arabia—and in Riyadh, although the scale was smaller than in the Eastern Province. Relatives of political detainees held demonstrations and sit-ins in front of the prisons where their family members had been incarcerated, sometimes for years, without ever being brought to court. Young Shiite activists claim that these Sunni demonstrations are inspired by the protest culture of the Eastern Province.

The most important of these Sunni protests took place in Buraida, the capital of al-Qassim. Hundreds of women and children gathered there week in, week out to demand that imprisoned family members should be freed or at least given a proper trial. In the period from 2003 to 2008 thousands of people were put behind bars in the context of the government's campaign against Muslim extremists. 'They also arrested dissidents and reformers on accusations of terrorism, because that was easier,' says the human rights lawyer Abd al-Aziz al-Hussan.

A few hundred demonstrators does not sound like very many, but according to al-Hussan, everyone followed their protests on Facebook and Twitter. 'This was no isolated incident. The people were demanding transparency and accountability. Everyone should be treated equally according to the law.' After March 2013 the demonstrations in Buraida largely came to an end. Al-Hussan thinks that the government may have made promises to resolve the issue. While the protests were still going on, they developed from time to time into attempts by Shiites to start a dialogue with their Sunni fellow-citizens. Hassan al-Saffar said, 'We have to be part of a national reform movement. The problem of the Shiites is just part of a larger problem in Saudi Arabia. The country needs a general reform and this would also mean the solution of the problems of the Shiites.'

The younger generation makes extensive use of social media and particularly of Twitter in its attempts to achieve a dialogue with 'the other'. After the crackdown on Shia protesters in 2012, for instance, a popular hashtag 'Kulna Qatif' (We are all Qatif) was launched, offering expressions of solidarity from Sunnis. How little most Sunnis know about Shiites emerged during a Twitter campaign in which someone joked that 'the Sunnis think that all of us here speak Persian'.

Joking apart, the gap seems unbridgeable. Until now all attempts, whether from the younger or the older generation, have achieved nothing because sectarianism is so deeply rooted. Even if Sunni liberals have occasionally spoken out about the repression in the east, they have generally not done so for long, out of fear of losing the support of their own, Sunni followers.[6] This attitude is even more the case with reform-minded clergy. The popular Sheikh Salman al-Awda has publicly rejected sectarian arguments and he regularly receives Shiite delegations, but the Shiites notice that there is never any question of him proposing any serious collaboration.[7]

Shiites complain that they regularly make conciliatory gestures towards the Sunnis, but that this hardly occurs the other way round. Jafar al-Shayeb makes no bones about his frustration, 'Look how many Shiite names there are on the [collective] petitions offered to the king, even when the issues are "Sunni" ones!' And according to another activist, 'We have done our best; now it's the turn of the Sunni reformers.' A typical instance was that during the Shiite protests of the winter of 2012 the Saudi Civil and Political Rights Association made no mention of the brutal behaviour of the security forces. Tawfiq al-Saif puts it even more explicitly, 'All the joint meetings of Sunnis and Shiites in Saudi Arabia were Shiite initiatives.'

In interviews with Sunni political science students at the King Saud University in Riyadh one also gets a sense of how profoundly the Shiites are distrusted. 'Of course they are trying to surround us and overthrow the monarchy,' Muhammad said in all seriousness. Naif endorsed his remark,

'A large number of Shiites from the Eastern Province go to Iran for medical treatment. You know what I mean …!' Even more shocking was the experience at a round-table conference in a prestigious Riyadh-based research institute. Professors, an ambassador and a former member of the Shura complain bitterly about Iran's regional expansion. The ambassador announced that 'We have already lost Lebanon, Iraq and Syria to the Iranians. This has to be put a stop to!' When the issue of Saudi military intervention in Bahrain was raised, the gentlemen were unanimous in their objections to the word 'intervention'. Did King Hamad bin Isa Al Khalifa himself not ask for help? Notions like these were entirely in keeping with Prince Turki bin Faisal Al Saud's endlessly repeated viewpoint. The prince, a former head of Saudi Arabia's intelligence agency (1977–2001), speaks unabatedly in the same breath not only about 'Iran's invasion of Syria' but also about the 'destructive influence of Iran on Bahrain'.[8]

No holds barred

For a short while at the end of 2012 and early in 2013 there were a few encouraging developments. The government closed down some rabid anti-Shiite TV stations, a Shiite was appointed to the Shura (bringing the total to six out of 150 members) and an interreligious dialogue centre was launched, albeit in Vienna and not in Saudi Arabia. The greatest satisfaction, however, came from the 'voluntary' dismissal of Prince Muhammad bin Fahd, the long-sitting governor of the Eastern Province, who had held the post since 1985 and who had been responsible for ordering the brutal crushing of countless protests.

But in April 2013 all the stops were again pulled out when an 'Iranian plot' was exposed. Sixteen Saudi suspects, some of them living in the west of the country, and a Lebanese and an Iranian citizen were arrested and accused of spying for Tehran. All at once the media were full of reports about this 'fifth column'. Like many others, Zuhair al-Harthi, a member of the foreign affairs committee of the Shura, did not mince his words, 'Iran has its expansionist project. Recent evidence shows that it has cells in Bahrain, Kuwait and Yemen. … Tehran intervenes openly, recruits agents and pays saboteurs.' He also made passing mention of the Lebanese

Hezbollah, although this organisation has nothing to do with Saudi Arabia, and he strenuously denies that his own country ever carries out illegal activities like this: 'Despite our logistic and financial resources, we don't engage in this sort of activity, for the simple reason that we are firm believers in not intervening in other country's affairs.'[9]

The radical cleric Muhammad al-Arefe added his bit by tweeting that 'the arrest of an Iranian spy network has added to our conviction that the Safavide sectarian government persists in its insults of Islam and Muslims'. Al-Arefe was referring here to the Persian dynasty (1501–1722) of the Safavids that made Shiite doctrine the state religion. In May ten more suspects were arrested. In Shiite circles, young and old, the accusations were firmly rejected. In fact, Saudi Shiites feel very little sympathy for Iran, even though there is always a chance that unrelenting discrimination may drive some of them into the arms of the Iranians. In the words of Jafar al-Shayeb, the Shiites tried to restore the matter to normal proportions. 'The government sees our problems through the lens of national security, and not as a political issue. Our demands are not at all excessive and it wouldn't cost much effort to meet them.'

Meanwhile, Sheikh Nimr al-Nimr, the hero of many of the younger Shiites, was still in prison without having been charged with anything. He was finally brought to court after eight months on charges including 'terrorism, violence against the police and inciting to sectarianism'. In the opening session of his trial, in late March 2013, the prosecutor called for a sentence of death by 'crucifixion', a penalty only resorted to for the most serious offences. Sympathisers and family gathered to protest against the charges, proclaiming that al-Nimr had only been involved in non-violent resistance. In October 2014 he was sentenced to death.

The war in Syria has added to the tensions in the Eastern Province. The increasingly sectarian character of the Syrian civil war, with Iran supporting the regime of Bashar al-Assad, has led to an even more blatant sectarianism in local Saudi politics. Sunni clerics in particular do their utmost to demonise the Alawite Syrian regime and its allies, which has had implications for Shiites in Saudi Arabia itself. Once again Sheikh Muhammad al-Arefe told everybody what he felt. Not only did he call for a jihad against the regime in Damascus; he also labelled the Shiites as 'unbelievers who must be killed'.[10] As a result, the Sunnis are now less likely than ever to build bridges with the Shiites.

Episodes of unrest, particularly in Qatif and Awamiyya, are a constant. In the hot summer months of 2013 thousands of demonstrators went on to the street once more. In June of that year the marches were in response to seven Shiites being handed down prison sentences varying from five to ten years because they had called on Facebook for the release of another leading cleric, Sheikh Tawfiq al-Amir. Demonstrations rarely occurred without violence. In the beginning of 2014 they again led to clashes after a Saudi court had imposed prison sentences of up to twenty years on seven demonstrators. They had been convicted of taking part in demonstrations and shouting anti-government slogans. Two police agents and two Shiite citizens were killed in these disturbances. Since the start of the major protests in March 2011 there have been more than twenty deaths, mostly of young people. An estimated 950 people have been arrested, of whom more than 200 are still detained.[11]

In early November 2014, Shiites in the Eastern Province were rudely confronted with the spillover of the Islamic State's sectarian war in Syria and Iraq. Sunni terrorists, several of whom had served prison terms in the kingdom for security reasons, attacked a *husseiniya* (Shia congregation hall) in al-Dalwah where Shiites were celebrating Ashura, one of their holiest festivals. Seven worshippers were killed, another twelve wounded. Saudi officials fiercely condemned the attack. Minister of Interior Prince Muhammad bin Nayef visited the families of the fallen officers to offer his condolences, but—more significantly—he also visited the *husseiniya* in al-Dalwah, a rare visit by a senior member of the royal family.

Even more significantly, the funeral of the victims was attended by an estimated 200,000 Saudis, chanting 'Sunnis and Shiites, we are brothers!'—an event described by some funeral goers as 'an extraordinary demonstration of national unity'.[12] Against the background of deeply ingrained anti-Shiism among large sections of the population, this show of solidarity was an important—and surprising—event. One swallow does not make a summer, however. For the moment, the number of open *takfiri* calls (that is, placing someone outside the community of believers) may have waned, but how long will this last? As long as the government continues to tolerate

sectarian hate speech from Sunni clerics and (to list just one more perti-
nent example) does nothing to change Saudi school textbooks which teach
that Shiites are un-Islamic, tension will remain. As one human rights activist said after the attack in al-Dalwah, '[On Tuesday], we saw the religious
rhetoric of Wahhabism translated into action.'[13] As more jihadis return
home from an ever-intensifying sectarian situation in Syria and Iraq, Saudi
Arabia will become more and more vulnerable to such attacks.

The unrest in the Eastern Province continues to be both regional and
sectarian in character, so that the protests are hardly likely to form a cata-
lyst for a nationwide movement. The few Sunni liberals who have spoken
out for the Shiite demonstrators have been gagged systematically. The
Shiites are clearly on their own.

10

THE COUNTER-REVOLUTION

KEEPING THE ARAB SPRING AT BAY

The uprisings in Tunisia and Egypt in early 2011 that resulted in the downfall of both these regimes came as a profound shock to the authorities in Saudi Arabia. Given the chance, they would have offered hospitality to the deposed Egyptian president, Hosni Mubarak, just as they had to Ben Ali, his Tunisian colleague. Since then they have endeavoured to limit the damage in their own country and elsewhere in the Arab world. Saudi policy is as contradictory as it is predictable, involving support for kindred despots against internal opposition—particularly in Bahrain—while backing opposition parties and insurgents, in Syria for instance, when required by the leitmotif of rivalry with Iran.

When Muhammad Bouazizi set himself on fire in Tunisia on 17 December 2010, the response of the official Saudi ulama was what one might expect. The grand mufti issued a fatwa in which he denounced self-immolation as a 'repellent misdemeanour and a great calamity', and in the same breath he labelled demonstrations as 'forbidden and dangerous actions'. They are 'non-Islamic' because they threaten the unity of the Islamic world.[1] The Ministry of Justice followed suit a week later, when the Court of Appeals in Mecca declared that participants in a demonstration could expect harsh penalties, including corporal punishments. Saud bin Faisal Al Saud, the minister of foreign affairs, added fuel to the flames by announcing that nobody should be in any doubt that the authorities would 'cut off any finger' raised in protest against the regime.[2]

To the extent that the protests in various countries continued and even increased in intensity, leading clerics began to adopt other, milder attitudes. Some of them, such as Nasir al-Umar and Salih al-Luhaydan, even revised their previous standpoints and called for people to support the opposition in Yemen and Syria. The prominent reform-minded cleric Salman al-Awda openly cast doubt on the legitimacy of the regimes in Egypt, Libya, Syria and Yemen.

In the meantime the government extended a helping hand to its closest friends among the despots by supplying them with large quantities of oil dollars to enable them to cope with possible insurgencies or, if that was no longer sufficient, as was the case in Bahrain, to lend them military support. The Gulf Cooperation Council (GCC), which is dominated by Saudi Arabia, proposed that a fund of 20 billion dollars be made available to the less wealthy monarchies of Oman and Bahrain. The kings of Jordan and Morocco also received invitations to join the GCC—in both cases, however, their answer was a polite 'no'.

Tunisia

Saudi Arabia adopted a different approach depending on the country concerned. In the case of Tunisia, it was one of the few Arab countries that refrained from congratulating the new regime after the handover of power. This was partly because it had offered hospitality to the exiled president, Ben Ali; at the same time, Riyadh was apprehensive of the possible influence of the fundamentalist but still moderate Ennahda party of Rachid al-Ghannouchi. In the past the Islamic philosopher and activist had in vain asked for asylum in Saudi Arabia and now some Saudi fundamentalists were celebrating Ennahda's success. Media run by Saudis such as al-Arabiya, *al-Sharq al-Awsat* and *al-Hayat* did their utmost to show the new regime in Tunis in a bad light (in contrast to Al Jazeera's reporting, transmitted from Qatar). Al-Ghannouchi himself was not exactly conciliatory, predicting at the end of 2011 that the Arab Spring 'would remove the emirs from the Gulf'.[3]

Official relations between Riyadh and Tunis are cool. At the same time, Saudi Arabia asserts its influence, as it always has, through the numerous satellite TV channels it has financed. Since the fall of Ben Ali newly set-up Islamic societies have played an increasingly important role. Some observers use the term 'Wahhabisation', and they are not far wrong.[4] Many of these societies work in close conjunction with prominent Saudi personalities and institutions.

Saudi preachers, moreover, are active especially in the Tunisian countryside, whether or not on the invitation of local branches of Ennahda. This may sound strange, but there is a simple explanation. 'Ennahda itself is divided: between religious preachers and pragmatic politicians as well as between its leadership's more flexible positions and the core beliefs of its militant base.'[5] The more pragmatically the party operates, the more it is alienated from its rank and file, and this offers fundamentalist forces a chance to fill the vacuum. Saudi Arabia is more than happy for this to happen. But after Ennahda lost the October 2014 parliamentary elections against the new secular party Nidaa Tounes, which counts many leftovers from Ben Ali's regime, better governmental relations are to be expected.

Bahrain

Bahrain is the only country in which Saudi Arabia has intervened militarily to rescue a friendly regime. (Yemen is a somewhat similar instance, which we will discuss later in this chapter.) The Saud and Khalifa dynasties have had close ties for many years, both through tribal and religious connections, since they are both Sunni regimes. An economic dimension has now been added and Bahrain is increasingly dependent on the 'Saudi infusion'. The physical link between the two countries is also important—the 25 kilometre-long King Fahd Bridge allows large numbers of Saudis to visit the capital of Bahrain, the much more liberal city of Manama where they can enjoy various leisure activities, such as going to the cinema. Official Bahraini media reported in September 2014 that a second bridge is planned which will reinforce links between the two countries.[6] Any threat to the status quo in Bahrain, especially if it comes from the Shiite majority, which feels itself discriminated against, causes alarm bells to ring in

Riyadh. Not only do Saudis fear that unrest in Bahrain might spread to the Shiite minority in the Eastern Province; they are always afraid that Iran will stir up trouble.

Their fears seemed to be realised in early 2011. The Shiites, who form some 60 per cent of the native population of Bahrain, were inspired by the protests elsewhere in the Arab world and went on to the street en masse. This is something they have done on other occasions in the past years, but this time the protests were larger and better orchestrated. In the middle of March the situation looked so desperate that King Hamad bin Isa Al Khalifa appealed for support from the Peninsula Shield Force, the military wing of the GCC. Saudi Arabia did not hesitate and dispatched 1,000 soldiers. Their tanks and armoured cars took up strategic positions in Manama. The United Arab Emirates and Qatar topped up the Saudi troops with a few hundred special police. The insurgency was crushed with much bloodshed, though without any direct participation of the foreign forces.

Both Riyadh and Manama pointed the finger of blame at Tehran. Not surprisingly, the Saudi government was backed by the clergy. Thirteen prominent ulama issued a fatwa consisting of a long list of allegations, denouncing the protests and warning of 'illicit schemes' by protesters. In the same vein, these clerics stated: 'This represents a forefront for a Safavi expansion that dreams of seizing the Arab Gulf and forming a Persian crescent.'[7]

The Saudi journalist Jamal Khashoggi, who regularly fulminates against the Shiites, summed up the government viewpoint in his own inimitable way:

Someone needs to convince the Bahraini opposition that they are not part of the Arab Spring … They believe that if the Egyptians can have a total victory, why can't we? If the Libyans can have a total victory, why can't we? … But Bahrain is different: … the society is divided between Sunnis and Shias.[8]

In other words the Bahraini demonstrators could not possibly represent a popular democratic uprising because they would only be a sectarian movement with a sectarian agenda. The fact that an independent investigatory commission, the Bassiouni Commission set up by King Hamad, found no evidence that Iran had been interfering did not make any impression in either Manama or Riyadh.

Attempts at a dialogue between opposition and government in the months after the intervention were sometimes blocked by Saudi Arabia. 'Our society may be ready, our government may be ready … but our neighbors are not ready,' a prominent Sunni businessman in Manama said. 'And if your neighbors are not ready and they don't like the deal you worked out, they can make it fail.'[9] At the time of writing, the protests are still going on, if in a diminished form, repression is continuing and Saudi troops are still a presence in Bahrain.

Libya

While it is abundantly clear that Saudi Arabia operated in Bahrain as a counter-revolutionary force, its approach to Libya was quite different. In that country it supported the overthrow of a regime with which it had had extremely hostile relations. In the past decades Muammar al-Qaddafi had missed no opportunity to taunt the Saud family and cast doubts on its legitimacy. In 2003 the crown prince and de facto ruler Abdullah was even rumoured to have escaped an assassination attempt plotted by the Libyan leader. Riyadh therefore sided with the insurgents, although its support was almost entirely verbal. The country played a crucial role in the Arab League, however, in adopting a resolution requesting the UN Security Council to set up a no-fly zone over Libya. According to reports, only eleven of the twenty-two member states were present when the resolution was passed on 12 March 2011 and among the countries that voted for it were all six GCC members.[10] The Saudis had lined matters up perfectly in the Arab League.

On 17 March the UN Security Council adopted Resolution 1973 which, besides setting up a no-fly zone, gave the green light to 'all necessary measures' to protect the civilian population in Libya. The latter supplementary clause went further than the original formulation of the Arab League. Saudi Arabia did not join Qatar and the United Arab Emirates in sending fighter jets to Libya, but it probably did supply the Libyan rebels with weapons. There was something fishy about this resolution. The debate coincided—in the same week—with the turbulent events in Bahrain. It is possible that the Obama regime hatched an agreement with the House of

Saud that if it gave its backing to Resolution 1973 then it would be allowed a free hand to intervene in Bahrain and that the United States would ensure that Qaddafi would be removed.[11]

In the meantime Libya has descended into chaos, with warring militias and two competing parliaments and governments. As the parliament in Tripoli is controlled by Qatari-supported Islamist groups, Riyadh supports the non-Islamist cabinet that is based in Tobruk and emanates from the parliament that was elected in June 2014. This government as a matter of fact has been recognised by the international community. In November, after (Tobruk) Prime Minister Abdullah al-Thani visited Riyadh, the Libyan Foreign Minister, Muhamad al-Dairi, said that Saudi Arabia was ready to train Libyan military personnel.[12] The regular army is fighting against Islamist militias which have taken over both Benghazi and Tripoli.

Yemen

In comparison with distant Libya, neighbouring Yemen always formed a more immediate threat to Saudi Arabia. Since the Arab Spring this has been even more the case. The country has a bigger population (24 million, compared with 6 million in Libya), is desperately poor and, after the United States, it has the highest gun ownership per head of the population in the world. It is in danger of dividing into two, while in the south it offers shelter to Al-Qaeda in the Arabian Peninsula (AQAP). If Yemen implodes, the consequences for Saudi Arabia are incalculable and millions of Yemenis would try and cross the border. The 1,800-kilometre 'security wall' currently under construction would do little to prevent this.

Saudi Arabia has interfered in Yemen from time immemorial. Like Bahrain, this country is practically a domestic issue for Riyadh—in fact the Ministry of Interior has been put in charge of these two onerous portfolios. Saudi interference does not only consist of giving generous subsidies to various tribal leaders, sponsoring Salafi institutions in those areas where Yemen's Shiites form a majority and occasionally intervening militarily; what is involved is a close partnership with the government in Sana'a. The Saudi regime interfered directly once again—and for a time successfully—in 2011/12 to bring an Arab Spring-style popular uprising under control.

Shortly after the overthrow of Ben Ali in Tunisia, a huge series of protests erupted in Sana'a too. The main opposition parties called for political reforms, but the younger demonstrators and the more active members of these parties, such as Tawakkul Karman of the al-Islah Party, a woman who later won the Nobel Prize for Peace, demanded the departure of the Yemeni president, Ali Abdullah Saleh, who had been in power since 1978. The fall of Mubarak on 11 February 2011 gave an additional impetus to the demonstrations. From then on, the slogan adopted was 'the people demand the fall of the regime'. In the middle of March a non-violent demonstration in Sana'a turned into a bloodbath, with snipers killing more than fifty demonstrators. At the same time a split occurred in the regime and the situation threatened to get totally out of hand. Saudi Arabia decided on an intervention using diplomatic means.

In the spring of 2012, on the initiative of Riyadh, a GCC proposal was adopted on the basis of which President Saleh would resign in exchange for total indemnity from any future criminal proceedings against him and his family. After a great deal of shilly-shallying he accepted this plan—he was given a full ten months to acquiesce to his departure. Compared with the fates of Ben Ali, Mubarak and Qaddafi, this ruling was exceptionally lenient. Young demonstrators came out on to the streets in protest against the arrangement which the Saudis had devised behind the scenes in close consultation with the Yemeni political elites. Not only was Saleh simply allowed to remain in Yemen; it was also feared that he would continue to pull the strings behind closed doors, which he did.

The unexpected, fast advance of Shiite (Zaidi) Houthi rebels to capture Sana'a in September 2014 placed Saudi Arabia in a dilemma. Although Houthis are not proxies of rival Iran, Tehran is definitely a supporter of the rebels. On the other hand, their advance has curbed the Islah Party, a branch of the Muslim Brotherhood which is considered a terrorist organisation by authorities in Riyadh. The Houthis are also firm opponents of AQAP. At first both Iran and Saudi Arabia welcomed the unity government agreed upon in September, for the few months it lasted. But as the situation in Sana'a worsened, foreign embassies closed. President Hadi, who first resigned, canceled his resignation and fled first to Aden and then to Riyadh. At the time of writing Saudi Arabia had launched an air offensive to reinstate Hadi. The country remains one of Saudi Arabia's biggest and most troublesome dossiers.

Syria

The way in which Saudi Arabia embraced the uprising in Syria is in striking contrast with its intervention in Yemen. First of all it was involved from the beginning in the latter country, whereas King Abdullah phoned Bashar al-Assad during the first protests in Dar'a (March 2011) to express the 'kingdom's support to Syria in the face of the conspiracies targeting its security and stability'.[13] And shortly after the initial bloody confrontations, the king had a three-hour phone conversation with the Syrian president. It was only at the beginning of August that year that Riyadh did a volte-face. The Saudi ambassador was recalled 'for consultations' and the king made a speech calling for the 'killing machine' to be halted and for a start to be made on reforms. What is the explanation of this about-turn?

It is plausible that it was provoked by the internal situation in Saudi Arabia itself, and also of course by Assad's alliance with Iran. Via internet, social media and satellite TV, a passionate campaign in support of the Syrian insurgency was now getting under way. Leading clerics had seized the initiative. The radical preacher Muhammad al-Arefe, for instance, depicted the Syrian president as a 'pharaoh' and urged 'the leaders of the *umma* [the Islamic community] to rise up and resist such barbarous deeds'.[14] Poets also contributed their share with poems urging the king to support the struggle of the Syrian rebels and demonstrations were held in Riyadh and Jeddah in which the Syrian president was called 'the dog of the *umma*' and the protestors chanted, 'We will offer up our blood for the King.'[15]

The king's next pronouncement at the beginning of August contained the first official criticism of Syria by an Arab head of state and formed part of Saudi Arabia's increasingly assertive foreign policy. Half a year later, early in February 2012, at a meeting with the Russian president, Dmitri Medvedev, Abdullah said that his country 'will never abandon its religious and moral obligations towards what's happening'.[16]

It had taken a while, but from this time onwards Saudi Arabia, along with Qatar and Turkey, actively started delivering weapons to the rebels in Syria.

This put the regime in an awkward situation. The conservative religious sectors were doing their utmost to summon volunteers to join the 'jihad' in Syria. Even Salman al-Awda, who was generally regarded as a 'moderate', presented himself as an advocate of the jihad, even if he used somewhat cautious language. 'If the killing continues,' Al-Awda tweeted, 'young people will no longer listen [to the government, which was not officially advocating Saudi participation in the jihad in Syria].' In response to the government's restrictive policy with regard to donations for the rebels, he warned that 'the donations towards Syria could not remain limited to a single channel; those who want to offer help will find a way of doing so'.

From the start it has been established policy, backed by the fatwas of the official ulama, not to send any Saudi jihadis to the Syrian war zone. Saudi Arabia has bad memories of jihadis returning from Afghanistan, who turned their attention to the royal family instead after 2003. Things were different in practice, however. Muhammad al-Qahtani, one of the country's best known human rights activists, described government policy as amounting to one of 'don't ask, don't tell'. In the course of 2014, after the extremist group Islamic State (IS) had, to use its own term, 'liberated' large parts of Syria and neighbouring Iraq, there were reports that at least 3,000 Saudis had joined them.[17] This is not so strange if we remember that there is not that much difference between the ideological principles of Saudi Wahhabism and IS.[18] According to most sources, Saudis, together with Tunisians and Libyans, are the largest group of foreign combatants fighting on the side of extremist rebels.[19]

In February 2014 the Saudi government started to realise that this development was undesirable in that it had the potential to lead to a 'blowback effect', similar to that which occurred when Saudi jihadis returned from Afghanistan. A new, harsh anti-terrorism law was passed, imposing mandatory prison sentences on jihadis returning from any foreign war zone. The measure coincided roughly with the sacking of Prince Bandar bin Sultan, the head of the Saudi intelligence service, who had also been responsible for the Syrian portfolio. This role has since been assumed by the minister of interior, Prince Muhammad bin Nayef, who had waged an effective campaign as deputy minister against Saudi jihadis at home and in Yemen, and has actually survived a jihadi suicide attack (in August 2009).

In September 2014, after President Obama's declaration of intent 'to degrade and ultimately destroy ISIL [as the US government calls IS)]',[20] Saudi Arabia was one of ten Arab countries that promised to support the United States in its fight against the newly established caliphate. Saudi fighter planes took part in attacks on IS. The much-publicised fact that a son of then Crown Prince Salman piloted one of the jets underlined the importance Riyadh attached to combating IS. What was evident was that the growing popularity among the radical youth of IS, with its claims to represent the truth of Islam, started to turn into a direct threat to the Saudi monarchy. One might wonder whether the Saudi authorities have left things too late in introducing stricter regulations. Due to its support for jihadi and non-jihadi groups alike, Saudi Arabia has overtaken Qatar in the backing it gives to the struggle in Syria, both militarily and politically. In the Arab world the Saudis are the most ardent advocates of a military confrontation with Bashar al-Assad's government.

There are various motives for aiding the rebels in Syria, but the most crucial one has been the rivalry with Iran. The Gulf states and Saudi Arabia in particular feel increasing concern about Tehran's growing influence in the region—even if they constantly overestimate it. Any excuse for restraining Iran is therefore welcome and the war in Syria is such an opportunity. Support for the Syrian rebels is generally presented in sectarian terms—as a battle between the 'true' (Sunni) form of Islam and the 'heretical' Shiites. Next to Assad's regime, the main target is his Lebanese ally Hezbollah, which is also an ally of Iran. For that matter, Saudi Arabia is increasingly interfering in Lebanon itself. In late 2013, the Saudis pledged $3 billion to Lebanon's army as a counterbalance to Hezbollah.

Iran

Distrust of the Shiites has profound roots among the Saudis. In the Arab Gulf states they are frequently referred to as 'Persian' (*Ajam*), implying that they are loyal to Iran. The reality is quite different—the vast majority are Arabs. Nonetheless, the dread of 'Shiite expansionism' is a constant Saudi mind-set. Even liberal intellectuals, like Khaled al-Dakhil, seem unable to free themselves of it: 'The Iranian project … is a sectarian project that would take the nation back to the concept of the infallible Imamate and the *Velayat-e faqih* upon which it is based' ('The Guardianship of the Jurist', the political model of the Islamic Republic of Iran).[21] Saudi foreign policy has also become increasingly sectarian in recent years. What is essentially a geopolitical struggle has been narrowed down to a religious one between Sunnis and Shiites. Saudi Arabia has played the sectarian card even more emphatically since the Arab Spring. The government is backed in this by the highest religious authorities. The grand mufti, for instance, said the Iranians were 'cooperating in sin and aggression' by backing Shiite insurgents in Yemen.[22]

In the short term such a policy wins applause from co-religionists in one's own country and elsewhere in the Arab world, but it comes at a price. The whipping up of sectarian feelings will only exacerbate the problems in countries such as Iraq and Bahrain and Arab Shiites will be reluctantly driven into the arms of Tehran, which was precisely not what was intended. It is also clear that rising sectarian tensions give more scope for jihadi-style groups in the vein of al-Qaeda and more recently the Islamic State. One trademark of the latter is that they are anti-Shiite.

Shiite political players, both in Saudi Arabia and elsewhere in the region, resort less and less to open sectarianism, and in this regard they would seem to be following the example of Iran. In Tehran one does not hear as many pronouncements about Shia Islam as about the religion in general. An awareness prevails there that the Shiites form a small minority (10 to 15 per cent) of all the Muslims in the world, so that drawing attention to one's Shiite identity would be likely to have the opposite effect to what was intended.

For a very long time Saudi Arabia has taken it for granted that the United States is on its side, and hence the beginnings of a cautious rapprochement between Washington and Tehran in the autumn of 2013 came as a rude awakening. The election of a more moderate president in Iran, the cleric Hassan Rouhani, offered Barack Obama an opening for a potential political solution to the controversy over Iran's nuclear programme. Obama has in any case never been an advocate of a preventative military strike on Iranian nuclear installations, such as Israel often calls for. King Abdullah was also a proponent of an attack on Iran. According to a leaked message to Washington of 2010 from the American ambassador in Riyadh, the king had repeatedly called at a meeting in 2008 'for the head of the snake to be cut off'.[23]

To the disgust of Riyadh, the P5+1 (the five permanent members of the United Nations Security Council, plus Germany) reached a six months' interim agreement with Iran in November 2013 (after which the talks have been twice extended). Saudi Arabia found itself de facto in the same camp as Israel; both countries condemned the deal as being much too lenient towards Iran. In Israel there was even speculation about setting up formal ties between the two countries. Foreign Minister Avigdor Lieberman said that discussions had been initiated between Israel and Saudi Arabia and Kuwait about establishing diplomatic relations, based on their common distrust of Iran. Daniel Levy, Middle East director at the European Council on Foreign Relations, even quipped 'Close your eyes, and you're not sure if it's an Israeli or Saudi speaking.'[24] Such an alliance, however, is pure fantasy, as it would provoke serious protests among sectors of the clergy and broad sectors of the population.

In the summer of 2014 the growing threat posed by IS appeared to have led to a further rapprochement between the United States and Iran, both of whom are hostile towards these Sunni extremists. There were even some signs of overtures between Iran and Saudi Arabia, which when all is said and done also views IS as a threat. In April 2015 Iran and P5+1 reached a framework deal which increased tensions in the region even more.

Egypt

'The enemy of my enemy is my friend' is a common saying in the Arab world as well as in ours. Developments in Egypt since the Muslim Brotherhood came to power in June 2012 are a perfect illustration. First, Saudi Arabia had to recover from the shock of Hosni Mubarak, one of the country's most reliable allies in the region, being set aside. When this was followed by Mohamed Morsi taking power, Riyadh was faced with the prospect of disaster. Even though relations were not immediately reduced to nothing—among other things, military relations between the two countries were too close for that—it was a case for Riyadh of being exceptionally vigilant.

Relations with the Muslim Brotherhood have not always been that bad—and to this day sympathy for the movement prevails among sectors of the population, including the clergy. In the 1950s and 1960s Saudi Arabia gave asylum to a large number of its members, who were fleeing persecution under President Nasser (and other Arab regimes, such as those of Syria, Algeria and Iraq). They found a niche for themselves in education and various transnational organisations, founded by King Faisal to counter the growing influences of Arab nationalist and leftist-leaning movements. After the Soviet invasion of Afghanistan in December 1979, many of them were recruited for the jihad against the Communists. Over the years hundreds of thousands of Egyptians have gone to Saudi Arabia as immigrant workers—altogether about 1.5 million at present.[25]

Relations became considerably cooler when Iraq invaded Kuwait in August 1990. Not only did some Muslim Brothers sympathise with Saddam Hussein's 'jihad against the West'; above all they objected to the arrival of American troops on Saudi soil. Protests also came from the indigenous Saudi population. 'Is America your God now?' the preacher Salman al-Awda fumed. In Riyadh an imam proclaimed from the pulpit, 'If a dog has come onto your land, would you invite a lion to get rid of it?'[26] After 9/11 relations were even worse. In 2002 Crown Prince Nayef, the minister of interior, said that 'The Muslim Brotherhood are the cause of most of the Arab world's problems and have done vast amounts of damage in Saudi Arabia. We have given this group too much support … The Muslim Brotherhood have destroyed the Arab world.'[27] It didn't help matters that, with Hamas as intermediaries, the Egyptian Muslim Brothers had allied themselves with the 'axis of resistance', consisting of Iran, Syria and Hezbollah. An absolute low was reached when Prince Nayef accused the Brotherhood not only of being behind the radicalisation of Saudi youth but also—completely without foundation—of being responsible for the wave of terrorist incidents in Saudi Arabia between 2003 and 2008.

Why does the Saudi monarchy feel so strongly about the Muslim Brotherhood? It is understandable that Morsi's visit to arch-rival Iran in August 2012 would have provoked irritation in Riyadh, but apart from that what was the problem? The simple answer is that the Muslim Brotherhood in power in Egypt represented a direct threat to the Saudi monopoly of Islamic political control and influence. Unlike the Brother-hood, Saudi power is not based on democratic representation (including free elections) but on the principle of absolute loyalty to the king. It stands for a docile, apolitical Islam. The message was clear—the sooner Morsi's government was overthrown, the better.

No sooner had the army seized power in Egypt at the beginning of July 2013 than the Saudi royal house sent the new regime its congratulations. In a phone conversation, King Abdullah let it be known that he was happy that General Abd al-Fattah al-Sisi had rescued the country from a 'dark tunnel'.[28] There was not a word of protest from Riyadh a few days later when the army gunned down dozens of pro-Morsi demonstrators. The new regime was immediately promised a 5 billion dollar aid packet (together with 3 billion from the United Arab Emirates and 4 billion from Kuwait). This aid was over and above the years of funding given to anti-Brotherhood forces in Egypt via political channels and the media. A few weeks later the king announced yet again that he stood 100 per cent behind al-Sisi. 'Let the entire world know,' he proclaimed, 'that the people and government of the Kingdom of Saudi Arabia stood and still stand today with our brothers in Egypt against terrorism, extremism and sedition, and against whomever is trying to interfere in Egypt's internal affairs.'[29] Half way through 2014 King Abdullah called for a donor conference to assist Egypt in its struggle against political Islam. He said that any country that did not contribute to Egypt's future would 'have no future place among us'.[30] In the meantime, Saudi Arabia had become the second largest foreign investor in Egypt, while remaining Egypt's major trade partner.

Twitter user @mujtahidd suggested that Saudi Arabia might have had a bigger involvement in the coup:

King Abdullah realised all too well that the failure of the coup would have been a disaster for the House of Saud. … The king was therefore one of the advocates of the use of unrestrained violence in putting down the protests. Not only did he support the coup, but he also persuaded others to accept the changes.

To cap it all, @mujtahidd suggests that Abdullah had actually promised al-Sisi a billion dollars a few days before the coup.

The Saudi government did not stop at just supporting the army coup in Egypt. In its new anti-terrorist legislation of February 2014 the Muslim

Brotherhood was defined as a 'terrorist organisation', and it attempted to persuade the Arab League—unsuccessfully at first—into taking a collective initiative on the issue. In March, Saudi Arabia, the United Arab Emirates and Bahrain recalled their ambassadors from Qatar to force this Gulf state to abandon its extremely friendly relations with the Muslim Brotherhood or in any case to cool them considerably. Qatar supported Morsi in Egypt with billions of dollars—which were handed back after the coup—but it continues to support the Muslim Brotherhood in Libya and Sudan, as well as the Brotherhood presence in the Syrian opposition. In November 2014 it was reported that Qatar had succumbed to pressure from Saudi Arabia and other GCC members and had promised to end its support for the various Brotherhoods. After King Salman's accession Saudi Arabia's attitude towards the Muslim Brotherhood somewhat softened.

The support for the military coup in Egypt and the extreme pressure it has put on Qatar are the most recent instances of the Saudi strategy of attempting to manage and reduce the impact of the Arab insurgencies in consultation with most of the other Gulf states and reducing the appeal of the Arab Spring domestically. Every available means was resorted to—from media campaigns ('If you want democracy, just look at the chaos in Syria, Egypt or Libya!'), to diplomatic pressure (sometimes backed by lavish subsidies, as in Yemen), or bribes (Oman, Morocco and Jordan) and even, in the case of Bahrain, to direct military intervention. Yet it remains unclear whether all this activity will make much difference in the long run.

11

AFTER ABDULLAH

THE PERILS OF THE TRANSFER OF POWER

Many Saudis would have liked to see King Abdullah stay on the throne for a long time. But it was not to be. On 22 January 2015, King Abdullah bin Abd al-Aziz Al Saud, custodian of the Two Holy Mosques, died in a hospital in Riyadh; he was around ninety years old.

On the surface the succession went smoothly. He was immediately succeeded as king and prime minister by his appointed successor, the former minister of defence and deputy prime minister Crown Prince Salman bin Abd al-Aziz Al Saud (b.1935). However, it is widely believed that the new king is unlikely to remain on the throne for any length of time—not only is he nearly eighty years old but there are also persistent rumours that he is suffering from serious health problems.

At this stage it is far from clear whether the new king will slow, or even reverse, Abdullah's liberalising reforms. But what is clear is his past history: he was the regime's lead fundraiser for jihadis in Afghanistan in the 1980s and in Bosnia during the Balkan conflicts of the 1990s. He is also known for his notorious remarks after 9/11, when he informed the American ambassador in Riyadh that the attacks were a 'Zionist conspiracy'.[1] He made the same allegation after Saudi Arabia's support for the Islamist fighters in Afghanistan and the Balkans backfired when jihadists returned home and initiated a wave of terrorist attacks in the kingdom—these jihadists, the prince maintained, were 'supported by extreme Zionism whose aim is to limit the Islamic call'.[2]

Prior to his death, King Abdullah had already made arrangements to ensure that his preferred candidate eventually succeeds Salman as king. In March 2014, somewhat unexpectedly, King Abdullah issued a decree in which he formally nominated Prince Muqrin bin Abd al-Aziz Al Saud (b.1945), the youngest living son of Ibn Saud, as 'crown prince to the crown prince'. It is true that Prince Muqrin had held the post of second deputy prime minister (a sort of 'crown prince in waiting') since February 2013. But by formally appointing Muqrin as 'vice crown prince' Abdullah curtailed Salman's powers as the latter is unable to appoint his own successor now that he has become king. Indeed, after Abdullah's death was announced, Prince Muqrin was immediately appointed crown prince.

Much more surprising was the appointment of Prince Muhammad bin Nayef bin Abd al-Aziz Al Saud (b.1959) as the new deputy crown prince. He stays on as minister of interior, a post which was occupied by his father for many years, the then Crown Prince Nayef bin Abd al-Aziz Al Saud, who died in 2012. In the person of Prince Muhammad a new generation of princes has finally reached the highest summit of power.

So on first sight everything has been arranged to guarantee a peaceful transition of power and continued stability in the kingdom. But will this be the case in practice? Under the surface some signs are visible of an ongoing power struggle, and while any disaffected princes have remained quiet thus far, there is no certainty that calm will prevail. And there are certainly enough among the thousands of princes who consider themselves eligible for the kingship to foresee trouble in the years ahead.

Thirty-six sons

The founder of the Kingdom of Saudi Arabia, Ibn Saud, was married twenty-two times while still adhering to the Islamic tradition of not having more than four wives at any one time. All these marriages bore fruit and he sired plenty of children. Nobody knows the exact number, but the most reliable sources speak of thirty-six sons and twenty-one daughters.[3] All these children in turn married various times and this has raised the total number of family members to around 7,000–8,000 princes and princesses. Exactly how many is a well-guarded state secret.

The male descendants—they are of course the only ones who are relevant in this context—are divided into thirty-five family branches, but not all of these are suitably qualified to occupy the highest position in the country. One important criterion is the origin of the mother, who must, for instance, be an Arab. Ibn Saud had married a considerable number of non-Arabs and that reduced the number of contenders straightaway. Sons of Yemenite or Lebanese mothers are also generally viewed as ranking low in the hierarchy—although this did not seem to matter in the case of Prince Muqrin, who has a Yemenite mother. All in all, this meant that of the sons of Ibn Saud who are still alive, only thirteen were candidates to ascend to the throne, at least on paper. And as Prince Muqrin is in line to succeed Salman as king, the remaining eleven have effectively been sidelined. For it is the third generation that will take over after them, as Prince Muhammad bin Nayef's appointment as deputy crown prince shows.

A family quarrel

Theoretically, one or other of Ibn Saud's sidelined sons could bounce back. But they are old. More to the point is whether their sons, the third generation, will acquiesce in the present plans. And that is anything but certain. Some speculate that the stage may be set for a real political fight within the family for the first time in decades.[4]

The past fifty years have passed with relatively few problems, but that was not always the case and there is no guarantee that it will remain so in the future. Disasters have occurred before. The second Saudi state (1824–91) disintegrated because the brothers Abdullah bin Faisal and Saud bin Faisal could not agree about the succession. A third party, the Rashid tribe, made use of the vacuum, occupied Riyadh, and forced the Al Saud family into exile. This catastrophe made a deep impression on the generations that followed and particularly on the founder of the present kingdom, Ibn Saud. Half a century after the war within the family he summoned his two oldest sons Saud and Faisal to his deathbed. 'Join hands across my body,' he told them, and 'swear that you will work together when I am gone.

Swear too, that if you quarrel, you will argue in private. You must not let the world catch sight of your disagreements.'[5]

Their father's warning fell on deaf ears. Ibn Saud was hardly buried before the two princes started to quarrel. There was every reason for this, as the successor, Saud, was a wastrel who was totally unfit to rule. Towards the end of the 1950s the country was as good as bankrupt, despite soaring oil revenues. Slowly but surely, Prince Faisal gained actual power in the teeth of fierce opposition from his half-brother. In 1963 their quarrel almost led to civil war, but a year later Saud finally admitted defeat—after Faisal had managed to persuade the ulama to issue a fatwa supporting his claim to the throne.

The following successions—from Faisal (1964–75) to Khaled, Khaled (1975–82) to Fahd and from Fahd (1982–2005) to Abdullah—occurred without any open bickering. The actual transfer of rule is perilous, however, to put it mildly.

Rivalry behind the scenes

In 2007 King Abdullah set up the Allegiance Council, consisting of thirty-four descendants of Ibn Saud, including a number of his grandsons. In theory this body would decide who would be the new crown prince after his death. This rule had already been broken with the appointment of Prince Muqrin in 2014 as 'crown prince to the crown prince', and though the Allegiance Council ratified the present succession it does not seem to have played any other role. Indeed, some observers saw this council from the start largely as a clever ruse by Abdullah to neutralise his prominent Sudairi brothers.[6] The latter are the seven sons from the marriage of Ibn Saud and Hassa bint Ahmad Al Sudairi, who comes from an influential clan in the Nejd, the central region of Saudi Arabia. The brothers and their descendants formed a 'family within the family' and have held crucial positions in the state apparatus for many years.

By institutionalising the succession, Abdullah aimed to reduce the dominance of the Sudairi group. In recent years he also removed various Sudairis from their posts, replacing them with his own confidants. His own sons Mitaib bin Abdullah, Abd al-Aziz bin Abdullah, Turki bin Abdullah and Mishal bin Abdullah were also given key positions (deputy minister of foreign affairs, deputy governor of Riyadh and governor of Mecca respectively).[7] Slowly but surely the position of the Sudairis was eroded, with the exception of the Nayef and Salman branches of the family.

Generally behind the scenes, but occasionally more publicly, rivalry grew between the sons of Abdullah, Salman and Nayef (d.2012). Of these sons, Muhammad bin Salman Al Saud seemed for a time to be the least likely candidate for the succession, not least because of the odour of corruption that surrounds him. The real contest was seen as being between Muhammad bin Nayef and Mitaib bin Abdullah.

Since 1999 Muhammad bin Nayef, nicknamed 'MbN', was deputy minister to his father at the interior ministry, and since November 2012 he has occupied his father's position. That appointment was the first serious indication that Sauds of the third generation were being readied for the highest office. MbN is generally viewed as the architect of the successful anti-terrorism programme in the post-2003 years. He cut al-Qaeda down to size in Saudi Arabia, after which the organisation fled to Yemen. 'The prince has built himself an impressive reputation in this area and that is what counts for the regime,' says Khaled al-Dakhil. He goes on to add, 'By coincidence this is also something that the Americans appreciate.'[8] In his role as interior minister, Muhammad bin Nayef is chief of police, of the notorious secret service (the Mabahith), of many special units and counter-terrorism commando brigades, of the border police and of the mutawwa. He is 'one of the few who can say that he has shed his own blood for his country,' says political analyst Sultan al-Qassemi, 'and that is a claim that is hard to match'.[9] Al-Qassemi is referring here to an al-Qaeda suicide attempt in 2009, in which the prince was slightly wounded.[10] On the other hand, Prince Muhammad is the father of the new, strict anti-terrorism law of February 2014, which criminalises not only violent extremism but also peaceful dissent as terrorism. Under his ministry liberal activists have been sentenced to long prison terms. A notorious example is liberal blogger Raif Badawi, who has been sentenced to ten years in prison and 1,000 lashes for insulting Islam. The prince holds hardline religious views and a friend of his once claimed his office still hires ultra-conservative religious figures.[11] Meanwhile, the prince has also been put in charge of the sensitive Syria portfolio.

For a long time Mitaib bin Abdullah (b.1952) was also considered a rising star. His career has largely been in the National Guard, a paramilitary force that does not fall under the Ministry of Defence. Initially its most important task was to protect the House of Saud against the threat of a coup; it was later also given the task of defending strategic locations, such as Mecca and Medina. The late Abdullah was himself the commander of the National Guard for forty-seven years and, besides his military activities, he also set up an extensive civil apparatus, including schools, housing projects and specialist hospitals. In November 2010 Mitaib took over the responsibility for the National Guard from his father, which he then proceeded to reorganise drastically, even momentarily mooting the idea of setting up a female sector. In May 2013 the king upgraded the National Guard to the level of an independent ministry, indicating that Mitaib's standing had increased significantly. Analysts saw this as an attempt by Abdullah to manoeuvre his son into a favourable position for the succession later on.[12]

But this was not to be. When the king died, his sons were more or less marginalised, whereas the sons of Nayef and Salman took the more important positions. Prince Turki bin Abdullah (b.1971) and Prince Mishal bin Abdullah (b. around 1970) were fired as governors of Riyadh and Mecca respectively (as were most of Abdullah's men in the Council of Ministers). Prince Mitaib has kept his ministry, for now, but he takes a secondary position in one of the two new super councils that were created in the cabinet under the authority of King Salman. One council oversees political and security affairs, and is led by new Deputy Crown Prince and Minister of Interior Muhammad bin Nayef. The other deals with economic and development issues and is presided over by the new minister of defence, King Salman's successor in this post and son Muhammad bin Salman (born c. 1980). Prince Muhammad, who is very young by Saudi standards, was also named chief of the royal court, a position wielding huge influence as it controls access to his father's palace.

Muhammad bin Nayef is widely considered, at least for now, as having emerged as the most powerful figure during the first stage of the transition from second- to third-generation princes of the House of Saud. But at the same time some analysts point to the role of the new king's son,

Muhammad, who became a special advisor to his father in 2009 when he was governor of Riyadh and continued in the same role when he was appointed minister of defence in 2011.[13] Prince Muhammad, who holds a BA in law and is rumoured to be the king's favourite son, is said by some to be the brain behind the shake-up of the power structure.[14] He also seemed to be the driving force behind the air offensive in Yemen.

MbN is perhaps the best known of these two powerful Muhammads because of his vigorous role in the struggle against Islamic terrorism and as an ally of the United States. But Muhammad bin Salman's new, big-spending ministry is an important one, which has traditionally been in the hands of the crown prince. Will these two men cooperate, or will a power struggle erupt between them? And there are many more currently unanswerable questions. Will the elder brothers of Muhammad bin Salman accept being passed over as their younger brother is elevated to this powerful position? Or will the sons of the late King Abdullah rebel against their unexpected demotion?

Quite another, but also very important question, is whether there are any reform-minded individuals among these powerful princes who might be willing to offer a bigger voice to the growing numbers of emancipated citizens. We know little or nothing about this, yet in the long term the monarchy will only survive if far-reaching reforms are carried out. It was the—admittedly cautious—reforming approach of King Abdullah that held his country together. The current king, as governor of Riyadh in 2007, came out against the imposition of democracy, according to a telegram to the State Department by the then US ambassador, published by WikiLeaks.[15] 'Changes have to be introduced in a sensitive and timely manner', he said. Democracy is indeed a far-fetched concept in the kingdom. The ministers of justice and of Islamic affairs he appointed after he took office are known as more conservative than their predecessors, if this is anything to go by. But in the end, no king will be able to turn back the clock to stagnation and strengthen repression—and get away with it.

'The Billionaire Prince'

Prince al-Waleed bin Talal bin Abd al-Aziz Al Saud (b.1955) is a man with many guises. Not only is he one of the richest people in the world but, remarkably, he is also an advocate of political and social reforms in his own country. Behind the walls of his company, for instance, men and women work on equal terms.

With his pronouncements he has sometimes trodden on the sensitive toes of more conservative Saudis. When asked to comment on the Arab uprisings in North Africa, he said bluntly that 'all the Arab countries that are still stable and where no revolution has taken place should wake up. They should carry out reforms without delay before they too become the subject of a wave of protests.' On the question of whether that was also the case with Saudi Arabia, he replied, 'Yes, no country is immune. Anyone who thinks he is invulnerable is talking rubbish.'[16]

He also regularly adopts the same stance as his government, as he did early in August 2013, after the military coup in Egypt which overthrew the Muslim Brotherhood government. A leading Kuwaiti preacher in Saudi Arabia, Tareq al-Suwaidan, was forced to resign from the religious TV channel al-Resalah (a part of al-Waleed's media empire, Rotana). Al-Suwaidan, who was the best-known face on this channel, had announced his strong sympathies for the Muslim Brotherhood and this was apparently sufficient reason to have him sacked. The prince issued a statement declaring that he did not appreciate 'aberrant ideas' like this, thus faithfully reflecting the policies of his late uncle, King Abdullah, who supported the Egyptian military unconditionally in their struggle against 'the terrorists'.

The prince captures the headlines more often, however, when the subject is business in Saudi Arabia. At the beginning of 2013 he again caused a stir. On the 2013 edition of *Forbes* list of billionaires the assets of this most wealthy of the Saudi princes were estimated at a meagre 18 billion dollars. The prince responded furiously, 'My assets amount to at least 9.6 billion dollars more'—and demanded the immediate correction of the entry. *Forbes* refused to do so, although a short while later it corrected the entry upwards by 2 billion. Al-Waleed broke off all relations with the magazine. Later on he even took the magazine to court in Great Britain over this issue. However great his real assets may be, there can be no doubt that al-Waleed is the wealthiest Arab of all and the only one in the top fifty in all the lists of known billionaires.

How al-Waleed calculated his starting capital is unknown. What is certain is that he is a sophisticated businessman who has built an impressive empire in a comparatively short time under the appropriate name of the 'Kingdom Holding Company'. His holding has a phenomenal list of assets at home and abroad. Hotel George V in Paris—worth 1.5 billion dollars at the time of writing—is one of al-Waleed's most costly and favourite purchases. Large-scale investments in a wide range of Western companies, such as Apple, Citigroup, Time Warner, Motorola, AOL, eBay and Disneyland in Paris have done him no harm.

The prince also has a reputation as a philanthropist, but the sums he gives to good causes are nothing compared with what he spends on his own princely lifestyle. Here is a small sample: a gigantic palace complex in Riyadh, with 500 TV sets in 371 rooms which are provided each week with fresh flowers from Aalsmeer in the Netherlands; more than 300 cars, including Rolls-Royces, Porsches and Lamborghinis; an eighty-six metre long luxury yacht; and a private Boeing 747 equipped with a golden throne. Until a couple of years ago he even owned a 'flying palace' in the shape of an A380 Airbus, valued at half a billion dollars, which included a parking spot for one of his Rolls-Royces, a concert hall, dozens of rooms and a prayer room with computerised prayer mats programmed to revolve to face Mecca.

The fact that the prince takes his religion seriously was demonstrated when he set up a sharia committee in his Kingdom Holding Company. And to get even closer to God, he is planning the highest building in the world in Jeddah, more than a kilometre high. The story circulates that the prince organises dwarf-throwing competitions from time to time, with the winner receiving a handsome prize. He does incidentally provide pillows to cushion their landing.

Does the prince also have political ambitions? In an unguarded moment, he did float the suggestion that he would like to be king, but this is not very likely to happen. Not only was his mother

Lebanese, which is held against him, but the rest of the Saud family are not exactly charmed by this man whom they consider as an eccentric. Rather more important is that it would distract him from his most important hobby—that of becoming even richer than he is already and attaining a higher position on the *Forbes* list. It must have distressed him that he fell four places in 2014.

12

THE POSSIBLE FALL OF THE HOUSE OF SAUD

A NUMBER OF SCENARIOS

The House of Saud feels under siege. This is indicated by the ferocity of its attitude to the Muslim Brotherhood, the vehicle of a rival, revolutionary and—judging by its electoral successes in the Arab world after 2011—popular Islamic ideology. This is why the Saudi regime was so enthusiastic a supporter of the military coup in Egypt that put an end to the elected government of President Mohamed Morsi, the leader of the Muslim Brotherhood party in July 2013. And this also explains its decision in February 2014 to label the Brotherhood a terrorist organisation, with suitably severe sentences for anyone supporting it in word or deed.

It was not just the Brotherhood, however, that the authorities saw as a serious threat; young Saudis who had gone to fight against the regime in Syria are also being arrested. The government initially discouraged militants from taking part in this struggle, but at the same time no attempt was made in practice to prevent them from going to Syria. Priority was given to bringing about Assad's downfall.

Thousands of Saudis did indeed depart for Syria, urged on in part by clerics who promoted the struggle against the Syrian regime to the status of a 'holy war'. Most of them joined organisations that have no time for the hereditary monarchy. Similar to what had occurred in Europe, it has finally dawned on the Saudi Arabian authorities that these young combatants present a potential threat when they return. They had of course had a similar experience themselves with the veteran jihadis of the wars in Afghanistan and Iraq who launched an armed struggle against the monarchy in 2003. Under the new, severe anti-terror legislation, combatants returning from Syria will henceforth be faced with long jail sentences. Notwithstanding these measures, a first jihadi 'blowback' occurred in the Eastern Province in November 2014.

Besides the Muslim Brothers and Syria veterans, there is a third category that is seen as a potential danger and which has become the target of persecution, namely that of human rights activists. Since the Arab uprisings, many non-violent activists have been arrested and given long prison sentences. They include university professors and lawyers who have been campaigning against human rights violations and advocating political reforms, such as the drafting of a constitution, the holding of free elections and introducing genuine transparency in government. Though unlikely, they could try and take over the lead of the currently unorganised mass of young people who vent their dissatisfaction on social media.

Muddling through

What are the potential scenarios for the near future or the medium term? Even though the monarchy already feels vulnerable, Muslim Brothers, Syria veterans and human rights activists do not pose any immediate threat. It is true that the country is run by an elderly political elite and that its economy is inflexible, but oil dollars can still purchase loyalty, though this might become increasingly difficult due to rapidly declining oil prices. Furthermore, and more importantly, life under the Al Saud may seem preferable compared with the wretched situation in other Arab countries. When interviewed, many Saudis say that they would like to see changes take place. 'But,' they always add, 'not in the way it happened in Tunisia where the transition is developing slowly and painfully, or as has happened in Egypt and Libya, with their ongoing instability.' And they would definitely not reject the status quo if it meant ending up like Syria with its horrendous civil war.

Social explosion

Nobody can be certain, but a lengthy recession in the oil market, whatever caused it, could spell an end to the Saudi monarchy. If oil prices do not recover soon, revenues will no longer be sufficient to fund extensive domestic sweeteners. In the medium term, the kingdom needs—according to some estimates—a budget break-even price of $175 per barrel in 2025. The pursuit of business as usual without serious reforms and with constantly increasing government outlays will only exacerbate existing economic and social problems and could easily lead to a social explosion. Karen Elliot House describes the mentality of the current, elderly political elite as being like a 'rabbit caught in the headlights'.[1] Doing nothing and biding one's time hardly bodes well.

Reforms—the king's dilemma

If the government genuinely started to listen to its citizens, this could also give rise to new problems. History teaches us that kings or emirs who do embark on the path of reform may end up with an unpleasant surprise. Reforms tend to lead a life of their own—a subject that Alexis de Tocqueville wrote about in *L'ancien régime et la révolution* in 1856. Was the guillotine not Louis XVI's reward for his modest reforms? The American political scientist Samuel Huntington later coined the phrase 'The king's dilemma' to describe this phenomenon.[2]

A similar course of events took place under the shah of Iran after he introduced his land reforms in 1963 (the 'White Revolution'). The king of Bahrain also unintentionally reinforced the Shiite opposition movement by promising concessions. Permitting a minimum degree of political pluralism has put the monarchy in jeopardy and the political crisis in Bahrain has not been resolved, despite Saudi Arabia's propping up of the Al Khalifa regime, including a direct military intervention.

In Saudi Arabia itself Crown Prince Fahd gave a striking instance of the king's dilemma at the end of the 1970s when he stated that 'Once we embark on this path, there will be no coming back. In the end we will have to face direct elections—nobody says we have to do that now.'[3]

Another variation on this scenario is that the king or influential princes would bow to the often-heard call for more transparent government. Any move in this direction would however be blocked by internal opposition within the royal family, because it would reduce the influence of the Sauds in affairs of state. It might easily provoke resistance from other more conservative factions in the royal family which in turn would lead to a serious crisis with unpredictable consequences.

Severe repression

Over the years protests from various elements in society have swelled, sometimes provoking the exasperation of the political and religious establishment. It is possible that this exasperation will at a certain point take the form of a backlash with all forms of social and political protest being prohibited or crushed. It would not be the first time that this has happened. In the early 1990s, for instance, King Fahd did just that with his ruthless assault on the Islamic Reform Movement. A comparable development is perfectly conceivable at present. Take the open criticism by influential preachers such as Salman al-Awda, who are calling on the government to listen to the voice of the people. It is unlikely that al-Awda will put up with being gagged. Will he be imprisoned yet again, as happened in the 1990s? And would that not result in his supporters going on to the streets?

It is true that there has been an increase in the repression of the opposition, but on the whole the response of the Saudi authorities has not been especially violent, with the exception of its treatment of the Shiite protests in the Eastern Province. This is certainly the case if one compares it to many other Arab countries. Incidents, however, can occur unpredictably and might trigger an unstoppable chain reaction. Another flood in Jeddah, with a large number of casualties, for instance, might be such an occasion. Or should a litre of petrol suddenly cost 25 dollar cents or more, instead of 16 as at present and people started plundering petrol stations.

Total implosion

The final scenario is that the country will implode. Saudi Arabia is unique among the nations in that it offers hardly any channels for participation by ordinary citizens, while not having any tradition of non-violent protest either. In a crisis situation, as in each of the scenarios described above, the risk is always present that differences of opinion will become so exacerbated that they may even lead to armed struggle. Violent opposition would be nothing new. This occurred in 1929 (the rebellion of the Ikhwan) and in 1979 (occupation of the Grand Mosque in Mecca) and in the post-2003 period when jihadis declared war on the state.

If the central authority should cease to function, a great number of differences will emerge that have until now largely simmered under the surface, kept within bounds by the popularity of the monarchy. Rival princes will then also go public and 'the family will no longer be a fist, but five different fingers'.[4]

Just suppose that the royal house falls and that the princes flee abroad in large numbers. The country would disintegrate, with the western region of Hejaz declaring autonomy from the rest. The east, with its oil fields, would come under Iranian influence and the centre would become a bastion of jihadis. Chaos and total upheaval would be the order of the day.

Even if Islamic extremists were to take power, they will also have to sell oil—you cannot drink it after all. The countries that would normally purchase it, however, would at the least feel grave doubts about a regime that would not automatically make it their priority to earn billions of dollars in oil exports to the infidel West. The price of oil would go through the ceiling, which would be a devastating blow for recovering Western economies and would also affect economic growth in the East. The price of a litre of unleaded petrol would rise to above €3.

The shock effect in the region and in the rest of the world would be enormous. No emir or king in the entire Gulf region would feel safe any longer. Bahrain would probably be the first to fall, followed by the other Gulf states. Oil revenues would go to revolutionary movements elsewhere in the Arab world, and one regime after another would topple, beginning with Saudi Arabia's neighbour Yemen. Jordan might come next, and the position of Israel would also become precarious.

A scenario like this is very unlikely at the time of writing, but in the long run a combination of factors such as we have described above can easily come about. It is no more unlikely than that the Saud dynasty will survive forever. Few experts foresaw the fall of the Berlin Wall, or that of the shah of Iran or of Hosni Mubarak in Egypt. The fall of the House of Saud is certainly no foregone conclusion, but the ingredients for an upheaval of this kind are certainly present.

NOTES

1. DO NOT FEAR YOUR ENEMIES

1. Madawi al-Rasheed, *A History of Saudi Arabia*, Cambridge: Cambridge University Press, 2002, p. 17.
2. Ibid., p. 16.

2. THE TWO-EDGED SWORD OF ISLAM

1. http://www.dailynewsegypt.com/2012/11/28/saudi-grand-mufti-slams-protests-as-anti-islamic/, last accessed 30 Mar. 2013.
2. http://english.alarabiya.net/articles/2013/02/24/268123.html, last accessed 30 Mar. 2013.
3. https://riyadhbureau.wordpress.com/2013/01/20/20131behind-clerics-royal-court-protest/, last accessed 30 Mar. 2013.
4. https://riyadhbureau.wordpress.com/2013/01/20/20131behind-clerics-royal-court-protest/, last accessed 30 Mar. 2013.
5. http://www.hrw.org/fr/node/105175, last accessed 30 Mar. 2013.
6. http://english.alarabiya.net/articles/2013/02/03/264031.html, last accessed 30 Mar. 2013.
7. http://saudiwoman.me/2008/09/13/prominent-saudis-sheikh-mohammed-al-arefe/, last accessed 30 Mar. 2013.
8. https://riyadhbureau.wordpress.com/tag/grand-mufti/, last accessed 30 Mar. 2013.
9. http://english.alarabiya.net/articles/2013/02/08/265035.html, last accessed 30 Mar. 2013.
10. https://www.youtube.com/watch?v=LX68g2fUh8s, last accessed 30 May 2014.

11. http://english.alarabiya.net/en/News/middle-east/2013/06/22/Fight-or-flight-Saudi-cleric-heads-to-London-after-calling-for-Jihad-in-Syria.html, 25 July 2013.

12. http://english.alarabiya.net/en/News/middle-east/2013/06/22/Fight-or-flight-Saudi-cleric-heads-to-London-after-calling-for-Jihad-in-Syria.html, last accessed 25 Mar. 2014.

13. http://saudiwoman.me/2008/08/22/prominent-saudis-sheikh-salman-al-ouda/, last accessed 30 Mar. 2013.

14. http://en.islamtoday.net/artshow-417–3012.htm, last accessed 30 Mar. 2013.

15. http://en.islamtoday.net/artshow-413–4568.htm, last accessed 30 Mar. 2013.

16. Ibid.

17. Ibid.

18. Ibid.

19. Ibid.

3. OIL, OIL, GLORIOUS OIL

1. See John Sfakianakis, 'Saudi Arabia's Essential Oil: Why Riyadh Isn't Worried About the US Gas Revolution', *Foreign Affairs*, Snapshot, 8 Jan. 2014, http://www.foreignaffairs.com/articles/140639/john-sfakianakis/saudi-arabias-essential-oil, last accessed 5 Aug. 2014. A 2011 Chatham House report warned that—on a 'business as usual' trajectory—the kingdom could become a net oil importer by 2038; see Glada Lahn and Paul Stevens, 'Burning Oil to Keep Cool: The Hidden Energy Crisis in Saudi Arabia', London: Chatham House, Dec. 2011.

2. Isaac Arnsdorf, 'Saudi Arabia's Risky Oil-Price Play', Bloomberg Businessweek, 23 Oct. 2014, http://www.businessweek.com/articles/2014–10–23/oil-saudi-ara-bias-risky-price-play, last accessed 25 Jan. 2015.

3. The interview was conducted before the oil prices started plummeting in mid-2014.

4. In early 2015, the central bank's foreign assets were $734 billion. See John Sfakianakis, 'Reading The Runes of Saudi Oil Policy', *Arab News*, 28 Jan. 2015, http://www.arabnews.com/economy/news/696071, last accessed 30 Jan. 2015.

5. https://members.gulf2000.columbia.edu/?p=310611 (access with password only).

6. Robert Looney, 'The Window is Closing for Riyadh', *Foreign Policy*, 1 June 2012, http://www.foreignpolicy.com/articles/2012/06/01/the_window_is_closing_for_riyadh, last accessed 5 Aug. 2014.

7. Sudeep Reddy, 'Saudi Government's Break-Even Oil Price Rises $20 In A Year', *The Wall Street Journal*, 31 Mar. 2011, http://blogs.wsj.com/economics/2011/03/31/

saudi-governments-break-even-oil-price-rises-20-in-a-year/, last accessed 25 Jan. 2015; Deutsche Bank, 'EM Oil Producers: Breakeven Pain Thresholds', 16 Oct. 2014, http://etf.deutscheawm.com/DEU/DEU/Download/Research-Global/2dd 759fe-b80a-4f07-a51c-dd02f4d384e5/EM-oil-producers-breakeven-pain.pdf. Also see Steffen Hertog, 'Oil Prices: Eventually the Gulf States Will Run Out of Power', The Conversation, 5 Jan. 2015, http://theconversation.com/oil-prices-eventually-the-gulf-states-will-run-out-of-power-35867, last accessed 6 Jan. 2015.

8. At the time of writing, oil prices had reached a five-year low. Andy Tully, 'Saudi Facing Largest Deficit in its History', OilPrice.com, 29 Dec. 2014, http://oil-price.com/Energy/Oil-Prices/Saudi-Facing-Largest-Deficit-In-Its-History.html, last accessed 30 Dec. 2014.

9. Robert Looney, 'The Window is Closing for Riyadh'.

10. Abdel Aziz Aluwaisheg, 'High Stakes of Energy Conservation in Saudi Arabia', Arab News, 24 Mar. 2013, http://www.arabnews.com/news/445868?quicktabs_stat2=0, last accessed 15 Apr. 2014.

11. John Sfakianakis, 'Oil Kingdom', Foreign Policy, 7 Aug. 2013, http://www.for-eignpolicy.com/articles/2013/08/07/why_saudi_arabia_still_rules_global_energy_oil, last accessed 6 Aug. 2014.

12. Sfakianakis, 'Saudi Arabia's Essential Oil'; Eckart Woertz, 'The Domestic Challenges in the Saudi Energy Market and their Regional and Geopolitical Implications', Norwegian Peacebuilding Resource Centre (NOREF), Policy Brief, Nov. 2013.

13. Aluwaisheg, 'High Stakes of Energy Conservation in Saudi Arabia', Arab News, 24 Mar. 2013, http://www.arabnews.com/news/445868?quicktabs_stat2=1, last accessed 15 Aug. 2014.

14. http://www.bloomberg.com/news/2012–12–27/saudi-arabia-must-review-its-oil-subsidies-former-adviser-says.html, last accessed 6 Aug. 2014.

15. http://uk.reuters.com/article/2013/07/30/saudi-metro-economy-idUKL6N-0FZ38O20130730, last accessed 6 Dec. 2013.

16. Keith Johnson, 'Running on Empty: Why Unbridled Oil Consumption in the Middle East Could Pose a Threat to the Region and Beyond', Foreign Policy, 23 Jan. 2014, http://www.foreignpolicy.com/articles/2014/01/23/running_on_empty, last accessed 5 Aug. 2014. Saudis consume three times more electricity than the world average. In 2012 electricity consumption grew by 9 per cent compared with the previous year, and peak demand has more than doubled in the last decade. See http://www.arabnews.com/news/598481, last accessed 30 July 2014, and Glada Lahn, Paul Stevens and Felix Preston, 'Saving Oil and Gas in the Gulf', London: Chatham House, Aug. 2013, p. 8.

17. This figure is based on the author's own calculations and is not undisputed. Other sources come up with other, sometimes even higher, percentages. See, for instance, *Arab News*, 19 Feb. 2014 and Kristian Coates Ulrichsen, 'Domestic Implications of the Arab Uprisings in the Gulf', in Ana Echagüe (ed.), *The Gulf and the Arab Uprisings*, n.p.: FRIDE, 2013. More figures can be found in Lahn and Stevens, 'Burning Oil to Keep Cool'.

18. Brendan Greeley, 'Why Fuel Subsidies in Developing Nations are an Economic Addiction', Bloomberg Businessweek, 13 Mar. 2014, http://www.businessweek.com/articles/2014–03–13/why-fuel-subsidies-in-developing-nations-are-an-economic-addiction, last accessed 12 Oct. 2014.

19. *OPEC Bulletin*, 2–3 (2013), p. 33. The prince estimated that the kingdom is currently consuming the equivalent of 4 million b/d of oil for power generation.

20. *The National*, 5 July 2013, http://www.thenational.ae/business/industry-insights/energy/concern-over-saudi-arabias-summer-diesel-consumption-surge, last accessed 5 Aug. 2014.

21. Woertz, 'The Domestic Challenges in the Saudi Energy Market', p. 3. For a balanced perspective, see Lahn, Stevens and Preston, 'Saving Oil and Gas in the Gulf'. The authors conclude that 'in all GGC countries the effectiveness of plans hangs in the balance, chiefly owing to governance challenges, lack of market incentives and unpredictable political support' (p. vi). In the kingdom it is particularly competition between KACARE (King Abdullah City for Atomic and Renewable Energy) and Saudi Aramco over the framework of investment in solar which has stalled things.

22. Jeannie Sowers, 'Water, Energy and Human Security in the Middle East', *Middle East Report*, 271, 44 (Summer 2014), p. 3.

23. Abdel Aziz Aluwaisheg, 'Runaway Water Consumption Alarming for Saudi Arabia', *Arab News*, 4 Aug. 2013, http://www.arabnews.com/news/460158, last accessed 6 Aug. 2014.

24. http://www.arabianbusiness.com/saudi-vips-clock-up-720m-in-unpaid-electricity-bills-report-558670.html, last accessed 15 Nov. 2014.

25. http://www.npr.org/2013/12/27/257654578/will-renewables-suffer-because-of-u-s-oil-and-gas-boom, last accessed 6 Aug. 2014.

26. http://www.bp.com/en/global/corporate/about-bp/energy-economics/energy-outlook/country-and-regional-insights/us-insights.html, last accessed 2 Sep. 2014.

27. http://www.economist.com/news/united-states/21596553-benefits-shale-oil-are-bigger-many-americans-realise-policy-has-yet-catch, last accessed 2 Sep. 2014.

28. Robert Kaplan, 'The Geopolitics of Shale', Stratford, 19 Dec. 2012; 'The

Geopolitics of Shale Gas', The Hague Center for Strategic Studies and TNO, Paper No. 2014–17; and Robert D. Blackwell and Meghan L. O'Sullivan, 'America's Energy Edge: The Geopolitical Consequences of the Shale Revolution', *Foreign Affairs*, Mar.–Apr. 2014 (and the nuanced response by Kristian Coates-Ulrichsen).

29. Note the rather sceptical opinion of the IEA's executive director, Maria van der Hoeven, asserting that the US energy security 'Golden Age' is an 'illusion'. See Syed Rashid Husain, 'Euphoria Over Shale Gas "Surge" Pointless', *Saudi Gazette*, 27 July 2014, http://www.saudigazette.com.sa/index.cfm?method=home.regco n&contentid=20140727212780, last accessed 3 Dec. 2014.

30. Charles C. Mann, 'What If We Never Run Out Of Oil? New Technology and a Little-Known Energy Source Suggest that Fossil Fuels May Not be Finite. This Could be a Miracle—and a Nightmare', *The Atlantic*, 24 Apr. 2013, http://www. theatlantic.com/magazine/archive/2013/05/what-if-we-never-run-out-of-oil/309294/, last accessed 5 Aug. 2014.

31. *Financial Post*, 18 July 2013, http://business.financialpost.com/2013/07/18/sau dis-feels-the-shale-heat/?__lsa=40ca-cb51, last accessed 5 Aug. 2014.

32. *OPEC Bulletin*, 4 (2013), p. 40.

33. http://qz.com/109505/the-billionaire-prince-who-says-saudi-arabia-is-in-far-big ger-trouble-than-the-other-royals-admit/, last accessed 7 Aug. 2014. Al-Naimi repeated this message during a Riyadh visit by the US secretary of energy, Ernest Moniz, in Jan. 2014. See *Saudi Gazette*, 'Al-Naimi Welcomes Use of Shale Oil', 19 Jan. 2014, http://www.saudigazette.com.sa/index.cfm?method=home.regco n&contentid=20140120193109, last accessed 7 Aug. 2014.

34. http://www.bloomberg.com/news/2013–07–28/alwaleed-warns-saudi-oil-min ister-of-waning-need-for-oil.html, last accessed 7 Aug. 2014.

35. http://www.theguardian.com/business/2011/feb/08/oil-saudiarabia, last accessed 7 Aug. 2014.

36. http://www.bloomberg.com/news/2013–07–28/alwaleed-warns-saudi-oil-min ister-of-waning-need-for-oil.html, last accessed 6 Aug. 2014.

37. John Sfakianakis, 'Is the Saudi Arabian Economy Productive?' http://sustg.com/ is-the-saudi-arabian-economy-productive/, last accessed 5 Aug. 2014. Also see Sfakianakis's critical analysis on 'non-oil exports': http://sustg.com/saudi-arabias-non-oil-export-figures-are-just-numbers-on-paper/, last accessed 5 Aug. 2014.

38. http://www2.kaec.net

39. Dave Eggers, *A Hologram for the King*, San Francisco, CA: McSweeney's Books, 2012. Quotes are taken from the Dutch translation, p. 40.

40. Ibid., p. 48 (from the Dutch translation).

41. Karen Elliot House, *On Saudi Arabia: Its People, Past, Religion, Fault Lines—and Future*, New York: Alfred A. Knopf, 2012, pp. 161, 169.

42. It is noteworthy that Saudi Arabia itself also has potential for shale development—though unlikely in the near future due mainly to technical problems. See Accenture, 'International Development of Unconventional Resources: If, Where and How Fast?' 2014, http://www.accenture.com/SiteCollectionDocuments/PDF/Accenture-Energy-International-Development-Unconventionals.pdf

4　THE TICKING TIME BOMB

1. Dr Khalid Al-Seghayer, 'It's Time to Listen to Saudi Youth', *Saudi Gazette*, 5 Feb. 2013, http://www.saudigazette.com.sa/index.cfm?method=home.regcon&contentid=20130205151998, last accessed 12 Sep. 2014.

2. Of the total population (30 million) some 9.4 million are non-Saudis. The estimates of the number of illegal immigrants vary greatly. In Dec. 2013 the government estimated it at 5 million, including foreign pilgrims who stayed on after the hajj or *umrah* ('minor pilgrimage'). See http://www.arabnews.com/saudi-arabia/shoura-tackle-problem-5-million-illegals-kingdom, last accessed 11 Sep. 2014. Also see Regional Mixed Migration Secretariat (RMMS), 'The Letter of the Law: Regular and Irregular Migration in Saudi Arabia in a Context of Rapid Change', Study No. 4, Nairobi, Apr. 2014.

3. The median age is 26.4 years. See http://www.indexmundi.com/saudi_arabia/median_age.html, last accessed 14 Oct. 2014.

4. http://www.ibtimes.com/saudi-arabia-feeling-pain-oil-price-plunge-it-has-enough-currency-reserve-last-years-1767238, last accessed 3 Sep. 2014.

5. http://www.eia.gov/countries/regions-topics.cfm?fips=OPEC, last accessed 3 Sep. 2014. At the time of writing, the oil price had fallen to a five-year low, leading to much less oil revenue for all oil-exporting countries.

6. Figures refer to gross domestic product (GDP) dollar estimates, derived from purchasing power parity (PPP) calculations, per capita. Source: International Monetary Fund, 'World Economic Outlook Database', Apr. 2014.

7. Sam Perlo-Freeman and Carina Solmirano, 'Trends in World Military Expenditure, 2013', SIPRI Fact Sheet, Apr. 2014, http://books.sipri.org/files/FS/SIPRIFS1404.pdf. The most recent figures about the 2013 defence budgets, supplied by London's International Institute for Strategic Studies, estimated that Saudi Arabia was spending $59.6 billion. This figure is said to be extremely conservative—placing Saudi

Arabia above the United Kingdom, France and Japan, and making it the fourth largest defence spender, with a defence budget that has increased by 111 per cent between 2003 and 2012. See http://www.iiss.org/en/militarybalanceblog/ blogsections/2014–3bea/february-f007/defence-spending-a132, last accessed 7 Aug. 2014; and Jonathan Schanzer, 'An Edge in the Desert', *Foreign Policy*, 3 Feb. 2014, http://www.foreignpolicy.com/articles/2014/02/03/an_edge_in_ the_desert_iran_middle_east_weapons, last accessed 7 Aug. 2014. Nawaf Obaid sketches a rather megalomaniac picture of Saudi Arabia's military ambitions in 'A Saudi Arabian Defense Doctrine: Mapping the Expanded Force Structure the Kingdom Needs to Lead the Arab World, Stabilize the Region, and Meet its Global Responsibilities', Harvard Kennedy School: Belfer Center for Science and International Affairs, 2014, http://belfercenter.ksg.harvard.edu/files/Saudi%20 Strategic%20Doctrine%20-%20web.pdf

8. For example, according to a report in *Saudi Gazette*: 'About 17.7 percent of the Saudis make a monthly income of less than SR4,000. Not more than 50 percent of Saudi families make SR7,000 a month … The stable incomes of about 15.8 percent of families range between SR1,200 and SR1,300. Those with high incomes of SR15,000 or more are only 11.2 percent.' See http://www.saudigazette.com.sa/index.cfm?method=home.PrintContent&fa=regcon&action=Print &contentid=20130829178506&simplelayout=1, last accessed 6 Aug. 2014. A 2013 study shows an increasingly sharp class distinction within Saudi society. See Mishary Alnuaim, 'The Composition of the Saudi Middle Class: A Preliminary Study', Gulf Research Center, Oct. 2013.

9. Ellen Knickmeyer, 'Idle Kingdom', *Foreign Policy*, 19 July 2011, http://www.foreignpolicy.com/articles/2011/07/19/all_play_no_work, last accessed 9 Jan. 2014.

10. http://www.youtube.com/watch?v=SlSBqgW5xx0, last accessed 14 Oct. 2014.

11. Daisy Carrington, 'Twitter Campaign Highlights Poverty in Saudi Arabia', 6 Sep. 2013, http://edition.cnn.com/2013/09/05/world/meast/twitter-campaign-highlights-poverty/, last accessed 9 Jan. 2014.

12. Other sources suggest higher percentages (16 per cent in 2013), for instance John Sfakianakis, 'On Saudi Employment: The Numbers Do Not Lie', http://sustg. com/on-saudi-employment-the-numbers-do-not-lie/, 16 Jan. 2014, last accessed 19 Jan. 2014. According to the employment minister, Adel al-Fakeih, 80 per cent of a total of 1,500,000 jobseekers were women, *Al Riyadh*, 3 Oct. 2012. Surprisingly, the rate of unemployment among Saudi women in 2013 has been pegged at 34 per cent, according to the Central Department of Statistics and Information (CDSI). That is up 2 per cent from the previous year. *Arab News*, 23 June 2014, http://www.arabnews.com/news/560096

13. According to CIA estimates, a total of at least 506,000 men and women will reach job age in 2015. They have to enter a market-driven labour force of 8.4 million, of which only about 1.7 million is now Saudi. See Anthony Cordesman, 'The True Nature of the Saudi Succession "Crisis"', Washington, DC: Center for Strategic & International Studies, 9 Jan. 2015, http://csis.org/publication/true-nature-saudi-succession-crisis, last accessed, 11 Jan. 2015.

14. David Ottaway, 'Saudi Arabia's Race against Time', Wilson Center Occasional Paper Series (Summer 2012), p. 5, http://www.wilsoncenter.org/publication/saudi-arabias-race-against-time-summer-2012, last accessed 10 July 2014.

15. Françoise De Bel-Air, 'Demography, Migration and Labour Market in Saudi Arabia', Gulf Research Center and Migration Policy Centre, Gulf Labour Markets and Migration (GLMM), 1 (2014), p. 9.

16. Abeer Allam, 'Saudis Confront Yawning Divide between Expectations and Reality', *Financial Times*, 22 Feb. 2011.

17. *Saudi Gazette*, 30 Mar. 2013, http://www.saudigazette.com.sa/index.cfm?method=home.regcon&contentid=20130330159057, last accessed 20 Sep. 2013.

18. *Al Arabiya News*, 22 Sep. 2013, http://english.alarabiya.net/en/views/business/economy/2013/09/22/Saudi-Arabia-deports-800–000-illegal-foreign-workers.html, last accessed 21 Sep. 2014.

19. Bel-Air, 'Demography, Migration and Labour Market in Saudi Arabia', p. 5. Also see RMMS, 'The Letter of the Law'.

20. *Saudi Gazette*, 23 Jan. 2014, http://www.saudigazette.com.sa/index.cfm?method=home.regcon&contentid=20140123193484, 30 Jan. 2014. Since then, deportations have continued at a steady tempo. See, for instance, *Business Standard*, 'Saudi Arabia Deports 370,000 Migrants Over 5 Months', http://www.business-standard.com/article/pti-stories/saudi-deports-370–000-migrants-over-5-months-114032000716_1.html, last accessed 1 Feb. 2014; and Ludovica Laccino, 'Saudi Arabia to Deport One Million People in Anti-Immigration Crackdown', *International Business Times*, 21 Oct. 2014, http://www.ibtimes.co.uk/saudi-arabia-deport-one-million-people-anti-immigration-crackdown-1471035, last accessed 2 Dec. 2014.

21. *Saudi Gazette*, 28 Oct. 2014, http://www.saudigazette.com.sa/index.cfm?method=home.regcon&contentid=20141029222697, last accessed 2 Dec. 2014.

22. http://english.alarabiya.net/articles/2012/12/26/257217.html, last accessed 26 Sep. 2013.

23. https://www.cia.gov/library/publications/the-world-factbook/geos/sa.html, last accessed 1 Feb. 2014.

24. http://blogs.wsj.com/middleeast/2014/02/03/saudi-labour-market-overhaul-comes-at-a-cost/, last accessed 1 Feb. 2014. Another way of boosting Saudisation rates is exploiting people with disabilities; see *Arab News*, 1 Dec. 2014, http://www.arabnews.com/saudi-arabia/news/668001, last accessed 2 Dec. 2014.

25. John Sfakianakis, 'Comprehensive Reform of the Labor Market in Saudi Arabia', 26 Jan. 2014, http://sustg.com/comprehensive-reform-of-the-labor-market-in-saudi-arabia/, last accessed 2 Feb. 2014.

26. *Arab News*, 11 Feb. 2014, http://www.arabnews.com/news/524191, last accessed 27 Mar. 2014. Equally surprising is the fact that remittances by expats in Saudi Arabia have gone up, year after year. 'Since the introduction of the Nitaqat nationalisation program in 2011, foreign remittances have reached SR383.6 billion, a 57.8 percent jump compared with the previous 10 years.' See http://www.tradearabia.com/news/BANK_251125.html, last accessed 26 Mar. 2014.

27. John Sfakianakis, 'For Saudi Arabia, Change in Fiscal Policy Should Come Sooner than Later', SUSTG.com, 28 Dec. 2013, http://sustg.com/for-saudi-arabia-change-in-fiscal-policy-should-come-sooner-than-later/, last accessed 27 Mar. 2014.

28. Knickmeyer, 'Idle Kingdom'.

29. https://www.youtube.com/watch?v=NMvCURQEhpM, last accessed 14 Oct. 2014.

30. As expected, in early 2014 it was reported that the building programme has been slow to get underway. 'Saudi Arabia Launches New Housing Scheme to Ease Shortage', Reuters, 13 Mar. 2014, http://uk.reuters.com/article/2014/03/13/saudi-housing-idUKL6N0MA17I20140313, last accessed 27 Mar. 2014.

31. *Saudi Gazette*, 17 Mar. 2013, http://www.saudigazette.com.sa/index.cfm/index.cfm?method=home.regcon&contentid=20130317157181, last accessed 18 Sep. 2013.

32. See, for instance, Carlyle Murphy's study, 'A Kingdom's Future: Saudi Arabia through the Eyes of its Twenty-Somethings', Wilson Center, 2013, http://www.wilsoncenter.org/sites/default/files/kingdoms_future_saudi_arabia_through_the_eyes_twentysomethings.pdf

33. Stéphane Lacroix, 'Is Saudi Arabia Immune?' *Journal of Democracy*, 22, 4 (Oct. 2011), p. 58.

34. Murphy, 'A Kingdom's Future', p. 49.

5. CHANGES BEHIND THE VEIL

1. http://saudiwoman.me/2011/04/03/going-back-in-time/, last accessed 30 Mar. 2013.
2. http://www.arabnews.com/saudi-arabia/shoura-council-have-30-women, last accessed 30 June 2014.
3. http://tifrib.com/abdur-rahman-ibn-nasir-al-barrak/, last accessed 15 Feb. 2015.
4. http://www.arabnews.com/news/560096, last accessed 30 Sep. 2014.
5. http://www.arabnews.com/news/550396, last accessed 14 Oct. 2014.
6. http://www.saudigazette.com.sa/index.cfm?method=home.regcon&conten tid=20130531160003, last accessed 14 Oct. 2014.

6. 'EVERYONE HAS TO LEARN TO THINK FOR HIMSELF'

1. Robert Lacey, *The Kingdom: Arabia and the House of Saud*, New York: Avon Books, 1981, p. 368.
2. http://www.newsweek.com/fire-wont-die-out-147083, last accessed 16 Apr. 2014.
3. http://english.alarabiya.net/en/life-style/healthy-living/2013/08/26/High-rates-of-obesity-in-Saudi-Arabia-behind-diabetes-and-heart-disease.html, last accessed 15 Sep. 2013.
4. http://www.bbc.com/news/world-middle-east-18571193, last accessed 14 Oct. 2014.
5. http://www.hrw.org/news/2012/02/15/iocsaudi-arabia-end-ban-women-sport, last accessed 14 Oct. 2014.
6. http://www.theguardian.com/world/2013/may/05/saudi-arabia-allows-women-sport, last accessed 11 July 2013.
7. http://www.arabnews.com/news/558416, last accessed 6 Aug. 2014.
8. http://www.ukcisa.org.uk/Info-for-universities-colleges—schools/Policy-research—statistics/Research—statistics/International-students-in-UK-HE/, last accessed 6 Aug. 2014.
9. http://www.kaust.edu.sa/media-relations.html, last accessed 8 Feb. 2015.

7. THE DIGITAL EXPLOSION

1. Some sources give even higher percentages. *Al Arabiya*, for instance, puts it at 41 per cent of all Internet users. See http://english.alarabiya.net/en/media/digital/2014/02/22/Saudi-columnist-urges-religious-police-to-monitor-social-media.html, last accessed 14 Mar. 2014. It should be born in mind, however, that the

figures are not all equally reliable. An interesting 'top fifty' of Saudi twitter users can be found here: http://www.an7a.com/112982, last accessed 14 Mar. 2014. See also Cooper Smith, 'These Are the Most Twitter-Crazy Countries in the World, Starting With Saudi Arabia (!?)', *Business Insider*, 7 Nov. 2013, http://www.businessinsider.com/the-top-twitter-markets-in-the-world-2013–11, last accessed 12 Aug. 2014.

2. http://mashable.com/2013/11/15/twitter-penetration-countries/, last accessed 13 Aug. 2014. For a recent survey of the use of social media in Saudi Arabia, see 'Getting to Know Social Saudis: A Closer Look at the Behavior of Saudi Users on Social Networks', the Online Project, Dec. 2013, http://theonlineproject.me/page/insights/20/getting-to-know-social-saudis, last accessed 11 Aug. 2014.

3. For a recent survey of usage trends of online social networking across the Arab region, see 'Arab Social Media Report 2014', http://www.arabsocialmediareport.com/home/index.aspx, last accessed 2 Dec. 2014.

4. The long-awaited verdict against people accused of causing the 2009 Jeddah floods was finally announced in Nov. 2014. The Court of Grievances issued thirty-nine verdicts that convicted forty-five defendants and acquitted seventy-eight others. The convicted defendants will spend a total of 118 years and six months in jail and will pay a total of SR14.17 million in fines; see *Arab News*, 1 Dec. 2014, http://www.arabnews.com/featured/news/668036, last accessed 2 Dec. 2014.

5. In Jan. 2011 there was another vast devastating flooding in Jeddah, during which ten people died, many more were injured, and millions of dollars in property was damaged. In late 2013, eleven people died in floods in various regions, and in Mar. 2014 a flood occurred in the northern Hail province, which is mainly desert, killing seven people. Most recently, in Nov. 2014, different parts of the country were heavily hit by torrential rains. Riyadh was paralysed. In the old industrial area in the capital, businesses came to a grinding halt. Almost every road in the al-Faisaliah district was flooded after just fifteen minutes of downpour. Warehouses remained shut in the afternoon as water seeped into many of them.

6. Garrat Nada, 'Twitter Sheikhs of Saudi Arabia', al-Monitor, 18 Dec. 2013, http://www.al-monitor.com/pulse/originals/2013/12/twitter-sheikhs-saudi-arabia.html#, last accessed 12 Aug. 2014. And Habib Toumi, 'Religious Scholars Dominate Most-Followed List', *Gulf News*, 14 Aug. 2013, http://gulfnews.com/news/gulf/saudi-arabia/religious-scholars-dominate-most-followed-list-1.1220096, last accessed 15 Aug. 2013.

7. Jonathan Schanzer and Steven Miller, *Facebook Fatwa: Saudi Clerics, Wahhabi Islam and Social Media*, Washington, DC: Foundation for the Defense of Democracies,

2012, p. 51, http://www.defenddemocracy.org/content/uploads/documents/facebook_fatwa_low_res_2.pdf

8. http://islamqa.info/en/, last accessed 2 Dec. 2014.

9. Habib Toumi, 'Saudi Mufti Blasts Twitter as Evil', http://gulfnews.com/news/gulf/saudi-arabia/saudi-mufti-blasts-twitter-as-evil-1.1401887, 21 Oct. 2014, last accessed 2 Dec. 2014.

10. 'Saudis Fear There Will Be "No More Virgins" and People Will Turn Gay If Female Drive Ban Is Lifted', *The Daily Mail*, 1 Dec. 2011, http://www.dailymail.co.uk/news/article-2068810/Saudis-fear-virgins-people-turn-gay-female-drive-ban-lifted.html, last accessed 3 Oct. 2014.

11. http://www.youtube.com/watch?v_OPXYNK 3ɒQ4, last accessed 2 Dec. 2014.

12. https://www.youtube.com/watch?x-yt-ts=1421914688&x-yt-cl=84503534&v=OpUUOYRLW3k#t=77

13. Rick Gladstone, 'Online Chats between Sexes Denounced in Saudi Arabia', *The New York Times*, 29 May 2014, http://www.nytimes.com/2014/05/30/world/middleeast/online-chats-between-sexes-denounced-in-saudi-arabia.html?_r=0, last accessed 30 May 2014.

14. Joshua Berlinger, 'An Anonymous Twitter Account May Be Starting a Quiet Revolution in Saudi Arabia', *Business Insider*, 22 Oct. 2012, http://www.businessinsider.com/mujtahidd-saudi-arabias-rebel-tweeter-2012–10?IR=T, last accessed 2 Dec. 2013.

15. Some of its episodes receive over 5 million views. For more recent figures and background, see Layan Jawdat, 'Laughing in the Kingdom: On Saudi YouTube Comedy', Jadaliyya, 11 Nov. 2014, http://quickthoughts.jadaliyya.com/pages/index/17256/laughing-in-the-kingdom_on-saudi-youtube-comedy, last accessed 2 Dec. 2014.

16. Reine Farhat, 'What are Users in the Arab World Watching on YouTube? [Infographic]', 19 Mar. 2014, http://www.wamda.com/2014/03/what-did-users-in-the-middle-east-watch-on-youtube-this-year, last accessed 15 Apr. 2014. Also Carlyle Murphy, 'Young Saudis Embrace Internet Satire, Rejecting Ultraconservative Islam', 23 June 2014, http://www.globalpost.com/dispatches/globalpost-blogs/belief/young-saudis-embrace-internet-satire-Islam, last accessed 11 Aug. 2014.

17. Human Rights Watch, 'Saudi Arabia: 15-Year Sentence for Prominent Activist', http://www.hrw.org/news/2014/07/07/saudi-arabia-15-year-sentence-prominent-activist, last accessed 1 Dec. 2014.

18. 'Sheikh al-Barrack, 'The Words of Ra'if Badawi Constitute Incitement to Apostasy' [Arabic], almoslim.net, 18 Mar. 2012, http://almoslim.net/node/162191, last

accessed 1 July 2013. For a longer list of those condemned, see Human Rights Watch, 'Challenging the Red Lines. Stories of Rights Activists in Saudi Arabia', 18 Dec. 2013, http://www.hrw.org/news/2013/12/17/saudi-arabia-activists-challenging-status-quo, last accessed 13 Aug. 2014.

19. 'Kingdom Amending Laws to Monitor Social Media', *Saudi Gazette*, 2 June 2014, http://www.saudigazette.com.sa/index.cfm?method=home.regcon&contentid=20140602207166, last accessed 11 Aug. 2014.

20. Saad al-Dosari, 'Is it Really Necessary to Curb Freedom on YouTube Productions?' *Arab News*, 29 Apr. 2014, http://www.arabnews.com/news/562651, last accessed 11 Aug. 2014.

21. *The Economist*, 'We're Watching You', 16 July 2014, http://www.economist.com/blogs/pomegranate/2014/07/internet-monitoring-gulf, last accessed 20 July 2014.

22. Kristin Diwan, 'Breaking Taboos: Youth Activism in the Gulf States', Atlantic Council, 7 Mar. 2014, p. 4, http://www.atlanticcouncil.org/publications/issue-briefs/breaking-taboos-youth-activism-in-the-gulf-states, last accessed 16 Mar. 2014. See also Abeer Allam, 'Saudi Arabia Cracks Down on Twitter', Al-Monitor, 20 Mar. 2014, http://www.al-monitor.com/pulse/originals/2014/03/saudi-twitter-crackdown-political-dissent.html#, last accessed 25 Mar. 2014.

23. The classic work on this subject is Evgeny Morozov's *The Net Delusion: How Not to Liberate the World*, London: Allen Lane, 2011. See also, by the same author, *To Save Everything, Click Here: The Folly of Technological Solutionism*, New York: Public Affairs, 2013. Media consumption of political knowledge—while informing through entertainment like YouTube comedies—can even have a demobilising and depoliticising effect, as is argued by Layan Jawdat, 'Laughing in the Kingdom: On Saudi YouTube Comedy'.

8. THE TASK OF ART

1. http://www.arabnews.com/news/657726, last accessed 2 Dec. 2014.

2. http://www.saudiartguide.com/, last accessed 6 Feb. 2015.

3. http://hyperallergic.com/55608/what-is-and-isnt-art-in-saudi-arabia/, last accessed 26 July 2013.

9. 'CURSE THE SHIITES!'

1. Though the smaller Shiite sects of the Ismailis (or 'Seveners') and the Zaidis are equally discriminated against, this chapter will only deal with the 'Twelver' Shiites.

2. Carlyle Murphy, 'Shiite Bias Claims Laid Bare After Showdown', *The National*, 26 Apr. 2009.

3. Fredric Wehrey, 'The Forgotten Uprising in the Eastern Province', Carnegie Endowment for International Peace, June 2013, p. 17, http://carnegieendowment.org/files/eastern_saudi_uprising.pdf, last accessed 15 Aug. 2013.

4. http://www.memritv.org/clip/en/3483.htm, last accessed 15 Aug. 2014; and Wehrey, 'The Forgotten Uprising', p. 17.

5. Wehrey, 'The Forgotten Uprising', p. 18.

6. One outstanding exception is the Sunni human rights activist Mikhlif al-Shammari. He is an outspoken advocate of equal rights for Sunnis and Shiites. He has paid a high price for this. Since 2007 he has been arrested repeatedly, declared an infidel, ruined financially and shot several times. In June 2013 he was sentenced to five years' detention followed by a ten-year travel ban by a special criminal court. The charges against him include 'annoying other people', 'consorting with dissidents' and 'sowing discord'. See Human Rights Watch, 'Challenging the Red Lines', pp. 24–7, http://www.hrw.org/reports/2013/12/17/challenging-red-lines, last accessed 1 Aug. 2014; and Robert F. Worth, 'Saudi's Lonely, Costly Bid for Sunni–Shiite Equality', *The New York Times*, 14 Mar. 2014, http://www.nytimes.com/2014/03/15/world/middleeast/saudis-lonely-costly-bid-for-sunni-shiite-equality.html?_r=0, last accessed 1 Aug. 2014. In Nov. 2014 he was again sentenced to two (more) years in prison and 200 lashes.

7. With regard to al-Awda, the 'sectarianisation' of the civil war in Syria is a complicating factor. It seems to have limited the possibilities for the sheikh's burgeoning attempts at fostering a rapprochement between the two sides. 'He is fearful that too much contact with the Shia in such a climate will alienate his Sunni base', as one activist in the Eastern Province remarked. See Frederic Wehrey, 'Syria's Sectarian Ripples across the Gulf', United States Institute of Peace, Peace Brief, 161, 15 Nov. 2013, p. 2, http://www.usip.org/sites/default/files/PB161.pdf, last accessed 1 Aug. 2014.

8. Project Syndicate, 'Has Iran Changed?' 8 Jan. 2014, http://www.project-syndicate.org/commentary/turki-bin-faisal-al-saud-assesses-the-continuing-threat-of-iranian-influence-in-the-middle-east, last accessed 2 Aug. 2014.

9. Zuhair al-Harthi, 'Espionage Cells in Kingdom: The Iranian "Fifth Column"', *Arab News*, 26 Mar. 2013, http://www.arabnews.com/news/446072?quicktabs_stat2=1, last accessed 2 Aug. 2014.

10. Frederic Wehrey, 'Ominous Divide: Shiite Iran v Sunni Gulf', United States Institute of Peace, The Iran Primer, 18 Feb. 2014, http://iranprimer.usip.org/

blog/2014/feb/18/ominous-divide-shiite-iran-v-sunni-gulf, last accessed 2 Aug. 2014. Remarkably, Sheikh al-Nimr had also called for Bashar al-Assad to go.

11. http://www.naharnet.com/stories/en/121838, last accessed 18 July 2014.

12. Rory Donagy, 'Sunnis, Shiites Unite in Saudi Arabia at Huge Funeral for Victims of "Sectarian" Attacks', *Middle East Eye*, 7 Nov. 2014, http://www.middleeast-eye.net/news/sunnis-shiites-stand-together-saudi-arabia-huge-funeral-victims-sectarian-attack-1956146358, last accessed 10 Nov. 2014.

13. http://www.middleeasteye.net/news/saudi-blames-al-qaeda-deadly-anti-shiite-attack-559410559, last accessed 10 Nov. 2014.

10. THE COUNTER-REVOLUTION

1. http://www.anbacom.com/news.php?action=show&id=19045, last accessed 12 Dec. 2013.

2. Toby Jones, 'Counterrevolution in the Gulf', Peace Brief, 89, United States Institute of Peace, 15 Apr. 2011, p. 2, http://www.usip.org/sites/default/files/PB%2089%20Counterrevolution%20in%20the%20Gulf.pdf, last accessed 29 June 2014.

3. Alain Gresh, 'Gulf Cools towards Muslim Brothers', *Le Monde diplomatique*, Nov. 2012.

4. See, for instance, Kristina Kausch, '"Foreign Funding" in Post-Revolution Tunesia', FRIDE, 2013, http://fride.org/download/WP_Tunisia.pdf, last accessed 12 Dec. 2013; and International Crisis Group, 'Tunisia: Violence and the Salafi Challenge', Middle East/North Africa Report no. 137, 13 Feb. 2013, http://www.crisisgroup.org/~/media/Files/Middle%20East%20North%20Africa/North%20Africa/Tunisia/137-tunisia-violence-and-the-salafi-challenge.pdf, last accessed 29 June 2014.

5. International Crisis Group, 'Tunisia: Violence and the Salafi Challenge', pp. i–ii.

6. *Arab News*, 'Second Bridge to Link Kingdom and Bahrain', 7 Sep. 2014, http://www.arabnews.com/news/626536, last accessed 25 Sep. 2014.

7. http://www.nationalkuwait.com/vb/showthread.php?t%D1% 81178129 (only accessible via password).

8. Justin Gengler, 'Bahrain: A Special Case?' in 'What Does the Gulf Think about the Arab Awakening?' European Council on Foreign Relations, Apr. 2013, p. 16, http://www.ecfr.eu/page/-/ECFR75_GULF_ANALYSIS_AW.pdf, last accessed 2 July 2014.

9. Gregg Carlstrom, 'In the Kingdom of Tear Gas', Middle East Report Online, 13 Apr. 2012, http://www.merip.org/mero/mero041312, last accessed 2 July 2014.

10. Pepe Escobar, 'Exposed: The US–Saudi Libya Deal', Asia Times Online, 2 Apr. 2011, http://www.atimes.com/atimes/Middle_East/MD02Ak01.html, last accessed 2 July 2014.

11. Ibid.

12. Ahmad Ghallab, 'Saudi Arabia Reiterates Full Support For Libya', Al-Monitor, 17 Nov. 2014, http://www.al-monitor.com/pulse/politics/2014/11/libya-chaos-saudi-arabia-support-ansar-al-sharia-terrorist.html#, last accessed 19 Nov. 2014.

13. Ahmed al Omran, 'Saudi Arabia: A New Mobilisation', in 'What Does the Gulf Think about the Arab Awakening?'

14. Al-Arefe said this during a Friday sermon on 6 May 2011; see http://www.you-tube.com/watch?v=Irwy9DZ1R48, last accessed 1 July 2014.

15. Satoru Nakamura, 'New Omnibalancing Theory and Tasks for Preventive Diplomacy: The Case of Saudi Arabian Foreign Policy During the Syrian Humanitarian Crisis', unpublished paper for the Gulf Research Meeting, Cambridge, UK, July 2013, p. 13.

16. Jonathan Schanzer, 'Saudi Arabia is Arming the Syrian Opposition', Foreign Policy, 27 Feb. 2012, http://www.foreignpolicy.com/articles/2012/02/27/saudi_arabia_is_arming_the_syrian_opposition, last accessed 1 July 2014.

17. Different sources give different numbers, but on the basis of several intelligence estimates there are at least 3,000 Saudi fighters in IS. See Jamal Khashoggi, 'ISIS Supporters Watch from the Shadows in Saudi Arabia', al-Hayat, 14 July 2014, http://www.al-monitor.com/pulse/tr/security/2014/07/saudi-arabia-islamic-state-support.html#, last accessed 16 Sep. 2014. Also see: Patrick Cockburn, The Jihadis Return: ISIS and the New Sunni Uprising, New York/London: OR Books, 2014.

18. Alastair Crooke, 'You Can't Understand ISIS If You Don't Know the History of Wahhabism in Saudi Arabia', Huffington Post, 27 Aug. 2014, http://www.huffingtonpost.com/alastair-crooke/isis-wahhabism-saudi-arabia_b_5717157.html, last accessed 16 Sep. 2014.

19. 'Convoy of Martyrs in the Levant: A Joint Study Charting the Evolving Role of Sunni Foreign Fighters in the Armed Uprising against the Assad Regime in Syria', http://www.washingtoninstitute.org/policy-analysis/view/convoy-of-martyrs-in-the-levant; Frud Bezhan, 'The Rise of Al-Qaeda 2.0', The Atlantic, 24 July 2013, http://www.theatlantic.com/international/archive/2013/07/the-rise-of-al-qaeda-20/278059/, last accessed 14 Sep. 2014; Aaron Y. Zelin, 'The Saudi Foreign Fighter Presence in Syria', West Point: Combating Terrorism Center, 28 Apr. 2014, https://www.ctc.usma.edu/posts/the-saudi-foreign-fighter-presence-in-syria, last accessed 14 Sep. 2014; and Cockburn, The Jihadis Return.

20. http://www.whitehouse.gov/blog/2014/09/10/president-obama-we-will-degrade-and-ultimately-destroy-isil, last accessed 15 Oct. 2014.

21. Khaled al-Dakhil, 'Saudi Arabia Struggles to Find Role Amid Regional Changes', Al-Monitor, 4 July 2013, http://www.al-monitor.com/pulse/politics/2013/07/saudi-arabia-iran-arab-spring-regional-role.html, last accessed 3 July 2014.

22. Glen Carey, 'Saudi Mufti Warns Against Sectarian Strife in the Middle East', Bloomberg Business, 15 May 2011, http://www.bloomberg.com/news/articles/2011–05–15/saudi-grand-mufti-warns-against-sectarian-strife-in-middle-east, last accessed 3 July 2014.

23. Ross Colvin, '"Cut Off Head Of Snake" Saudis Told US On Iran', Reuters, 29 Nov. 2010, http://www.reuters.com/article/2010/11/29/us-wikileaks-iran-saudis-idUSTRE6AS02B20101129, last accessed 2 Feb. 2013.

24. Helene Cooper, 'Converging Interests May Lead to Cooperation between Israel and Gulf States', *The New York Times*, 31 Mar. 2014, http://www.nytimes.com/2014/04/01/world/middleeast/converging-interests-may-lead-to-cooperation-between-israel-and-gulf-states.html?_r=0, last accessed 3 July 2014; Bernard Haykal, 'Middle East Frenemies', Project Syndicate, 13 Dec. 2013, http://www.project-syndicate.org/commentary/bernard-haykel-emphasizes-the-limits-to-saudi-israeli-cooperation-in-confronting-iran; http://www.ynetnews.com/articles/0,7340,L-4510125,00.html, last accessed 3 July 2014.

25. Yasmine Farouk, 'More than Money: Post-Mubarak Egypt, Saudi Arabia, and the Gulf', Gulf Research Center: GRC Gulf Paper, Apr. 2014, http://www.grc.net/data/contents/uploads/Egypt_Money_new_12–05–14_4667.pdf, last accessed 16 Sep. 2014.

26. James Piscatori, 'Religion and Realpolitik: Islamic Responses to the Gulf War', in James Piscatori (ed.), *Islamic Fundamentalism and the Gulf Crisis*, Chicago: The American Academy of Arts and Sciences, 1991, p. 10.

27. Gresh, 'Gulf Cools towards Muslim Brothers'.

28. Sultan Saooud Al Qassemi, 'Gulf States Embrace Post-Brotherhood Egypt', Al-Monitor, 10 July 2013, http://www.al-monitor.com/pulse/originals/2013/07/gulf-states-egypt-muslim-brotherhood.html, last accessed 1 July 2014.

29. David Hearst, 'Why Saudi Arabia is Taking a Risk by Backing the Egyptian Coup', *The Guardian*, 20 Aug. 2013, http://www.theguardian.com/commentisfree/2013/aug/20/saudi-arabia-coup-egypt, last accessed 1 July 2014.

30. Simeon Kerr, 'Saudi Arabia Calls on Region to Assist Egypt', *Financial Times*, 3 June 2014, http://www.ft.com/intl/cms/s/0/68bd01f0-eb53–11e3-bab6–00144feabdc0.html#axzz3DTVgC700, last accessed 30 June 2014.

11. AFTER ABDULLAH

1. Simon Henderson, 'The Man Who Would be King', *Foreign Policy*, 10 Apr. 2012, http://foreignpolicy.com/2012/04/10/the-man-who-would-be-king

2. David Andrew Weinberg, 'King Salman's Shady History', *Foreign Policy*, 27 Jan. 2015, http://foreignpolicy.com/2015/01/27/king-salmans-shady-history-saudi-arabia-jihadi-ties/, last accessed 6 Feb. 2015.

3. See, for instance, Stig Stenslie, *Regime Stability in Saudi Arabia: The Challenge of Succession*, New York: Routledge, 2012.

4. F. Gregory Gause III, 'Saudi Arabia's Game of Thrones: King Salman Amasses Power', *Foreign Affairs*, 2 Feb. 2015, http://www.foreignaffairs.com/articles/1428 42/f-gregory-gause-iii/saudi-arabias-game-of-thrones, last accessed 6 Feb. 2015.

5. House, *On Saudi Arabia*, p. 210.

6. Fouad al-Ibrahim, 'Undermining the Sudairi Clan: The King Manages the Power Struggle', Al Akhbar English, 16 May 2014, http://english.al-akhbar.com/node/19798, last accessed 6 Feb. 2015; Nabil Mouline, 'Power and Generational Transition in Saudi Arabia', *Critique internationale*, 46 (Apr.–June 2010), pp. 125–46.

7. Joseph Kéchichian, 'Saudis Smooth Rough Succession Issues', Gulfnews.com, 2 Apr. 2014, http://gulfnews.com/opinions/columnists/saudis-smooth-rough-succession-issues-1.1312917, last accessed 28 Aug. 2014. For more on the succession issue, see Bruce Riedel, 'Saudi King's Sons Well-Placed for Transition', Al-Monitor, 30 May 2014, http://www.al-monitor.com/pulse/tr/originals/2014/05/saudi-transition-kings-sons-well-place.html#; Michael Herb, 'The Saudi Succession and Challenges Facing Saudi Arabia,' NOREF, Aug. 2014, http://www.peacebuilding. no/var/ezflow_site/storage/original/application/606cfa31b5e4c02fe414bfaa 82d79152.pdf; Jean Aziz, 'Changes in Saudi Defense Ministry a Matter of Family Politics', Al-Monitor, 27 May 2014, http://www.al-monitor.com/pulse/ru/originals/2014/05/reshufflings-saudi-defense-ministry-abdullah.html; Simon Henderson, 'After King Abdullah: Succession in Saudi Arabia', The Washington Institute for Near East Policy, Policy Focus no. 96, Aug. 2009, http://www.washingtoninstitute.org/uploads/Documents/pubs/PolicyFocus96_Henderson.pdf; and Simon Henderson, 'Saudi Arabia's Family Feud', *Foreign Policy*, 7 July 2014, http://www.washingtoninstitute.org/policy-analysis/view/saudi-arabias-family-feud; all last accessed 22 Sep. 2014.

8. As quoted in Glen Carey, 'Saudi Next Generation Has U.S. Imprint as King Picks Leaders', Bloomberg, 6 Mar. 2013, http://www.bloomberg.com/news/arti-

cles/2013–03–05/saudi-next-generation-has-u-s-imprint-as-king-grooms-successors, last accessed 28 Aug. 2014.

9. As quoted in *Gulf States Newsletter* 33, 863, 23 Oct. 2009, http://www.scribd.com/doc/43649166/Assassination-attempt-improves-Mohammed-Bin-Nayef-s-fortunes-GSN-Issue-863–23-October-2009, last accessed 28 Aug. 2014.

10. This was not the only assassination attempt. Several others took place, including one during a visit to Yemen. See Al Bawaba News, 'Mohammed bin Nayef: A King in Waiting', 27 Jan. 2015, http://www.albawaba.com/news/mohammed-bin-nayef-king-waiting-649420, last accessed 6 Feb. 2015.

11. 'Mohammed bin Nayef: A King in Waiting'.

12. Bruce Riedel, 'Saudi King's Well-placed for Transition', Al-Monitor, 30 May 2014, http://www.al-monitor.com/pulse/tr/originals/2014/05/saudi-transition-kings-sons-well-place.html, last accessed 28 Aug. 2014; Jean Aziz, 'Changes in Saudi Defense Ministry a Matter of Family Politics', Al-Monitor, 27 May 2014, http://www.al-monitor.com/pulse/ru/originals/2014/05/reshufflings-saudi-defense-ministry-abdullah.html, last accessed 28 Aug. 2014.

13. Al Arabiya News, 'Profile of Prince Mohammed bin Salman bin Abdulaziz Al Saud', 27 Jan. 2015, http://english.alarabiya.net/en/perspective/profiles/2015/01/27/Profile-Prince-Mohammed-bin-Salman-bin-Abdulaziz-Al-Saud.html, last accessed 6 Feb. 2015.

14. http://www.washingtonpost.com/opinions/david-ignatius-reshuffling-the-house-of-saud/2015/02/03/6b35c8b8-abec-11e4-abe8-e1ef60ca26de_story.html, last accessed 6 Feb. 2015.

15. https://wikileaks.org/plusd/cables/07RIYADH651_a.html

16. http://www.itv.com/news/topic/prince-al-waleed-bin-talal/, last accessed 27 Aug. 2014.

12. THE POSSIBLE FALL OF THE HOUSE OF SAUD

1. We have made grateful use here of House, *On Saudi Arabia*, p. 219.

2. Samuel Huntington, *Political Order in Changing Societies*, New Haven: Yale University Press, 1968.

3. Robert Lacey, *Inside the Kingdom: Kings, Clerics, Modernists, Terrorists and the Struggle for Saudi Arabia*, London: Arrow Books, 2010, pp. 48–9.

4. Interview with a high-ranking employee of Aramco, 28 Mar. 2013.

FURTHER READING

Aarts, Paul, 'Maintaining Authoritarianism: The Jerky Path of Political Reform in Saudi Arabia', *Orient*, 1 (2011), pp. 29–42.

Aarts, Paul and Gerd Nonneman (eds), *Saudi Arabia in the Balance: Political Economy, Society, Foreign Affairs*, London: Hurst, 2005.

AbuKhalil, As'ad, *The Battle for Saudi Arabia: Royalty, Fundamentalism, and Global Power*, New York: Seven Stories Press, 2004.

Algar, Hamid, *Wahhabism: A Critical Essay*, Oneonta, NY: Islamic Publications International, 2002.

Alsanea, Rajaa, *Girls of Riyadh*, London: Fig Tree/Penguin Books, 2007.

Ayoob, Mohammed and Hassan Kosebalaban (eds), *Religion and Politics in Saudi Arabia: Wahhabism and the State*, Boulder/London: Lynne Rienner, 2009.

Bradley, John R., *Saudi Arabia Exposed: Inside a Kingdom in Crisis*, New York: Palgrave Macmillan, 2005.

Bronson, Rachel, *Thicker than Oil: America's Uneasy Partnership with Saudi Arabia*, New York: Oxford University Press, 2006.

Champion, Daryl, *The Paradoxical Kingdom. Saudi Arabia and the Momentum of Reform*, London: Hurst, 2003.

Coates Ulrichsen, Kristian, 'Domestic Implications of the Arab Uprisings in the Gulf', in Ana Echagüe (ed.), *The Gulf States and the Arab Uprisings*, Madrid: FRIDE, 2013, pp. 35–46.

Commins, David, *The Wahhabi Mission and Saudi Arabia*, London: I.B. Tauris, 2005.

Cordesman, Anthony H. and Nawaf Obaid, *National Security in Saudi Arabia*, Santa Barbara, CA: Praeger Security International, 2005.

Davidson, Christopher, *After the Sheikhs: The Coming Collapse of the Gulf Monarchies*, London: Hurst, 2012.

FURTHER READING

Delong-Bas, Natana J., *Wahhabi Islam: From Revival and Reform to Global Jihad*, New York: Oxford University Press, 2004.

Gause, F. Gregory III, 'Kings for All Seasons: How the Middle East's Monarchies Survived the Arab Spring', Brookings Doha Center Analysis Paper, no. 8, Sep. 2013.

Hammond, Andrew, *The Islamic Utopia: The Illusion of Reform in Saudi Arabia*, New York: PlutoPress, 2012.

Haykel, Bernard, Thomas Hegghammer and Stephane Lacroix (eds), *Saudi Arabia in Transition: Insights on Social, Political, Economic and Religious Change*, Cambridge: Cambridge University Press, 2015.

Hegghammer, Thomas, *Jihad in Saudi Arabia: Violence and Pan-Islamism since 1979*, Cambridge: Cambridge University Press, 2010.

Hertog, Steffen, *Princes, Brokers, and Bureaucrats: Oil and the State in Saudi Arabia*, Ithaca, NY: Cornell University Press, 2010.

House, Karen Elliot, *On Arabia: Its People, Past, Religion, Fault Lines—and Future*, New York: Alfred Knopf, 2012.

Ibrahim, Fouad, *The Shi'is of Saudi Arabia*, London: Saqi, 2006.

Jones, Toby, *Desert Kingdom: How Oil and Water Forged Modern Saudi Arabia*, Cambridge, MA: Harvard University Press, 2010.

Kéchichian, Joseph A., *Legal and Political Reforms in Sa'udi Arabia*, London: Routledge, 2013.

Lacey, Robert, *Inside the Kingdom: Kings, Clerics, Modernists, Terrorists and the Struggle for Saudi Arabia*, London: Arrow Books, 2010.

———— *The Kingdom: Arabia and the House of Saud*, London: Hutchinson, 1981.

Lacroix, Stéphane, *Awakening Islam: The Politics of Religious Dissent in Contemporary Saudi Arabia*, Cambridge, MA: Harvard University Press, 2011.

Lippman, Thomas W., *Inside the Mirage: America's Fragile Partnership with Saudi Arabia*, Boulder, CO: Westview Press, 2004.

Mathiessen, Toby, *The Other Saudis: Shiism, Dissent and Sectarianism*, Cambridge: Cambridge University Press, 2014.

———— *Sectarian Gulf: Bahrain, Saudi Arabia, and the Arab Spring that Wasn't*, Stanford, CA: Stanford University Press, 2013.

Meijer, Roel and Paul Aarts (eds), 'Saudi Arabia between Conservatism, Accommodation and Reform', The Hague: Clingendael, 2012.

Ménoret, Pascal, *The Saudi Engima: A History*, London/New York: Zed Books, 2005.

———— *Joyriding in Riyadh: Oil, Urbanism and Road Revolt*, Cambridge: Cambridge University Press, 2014.

Murphy, Carlyle, 'A Kingdom's Future: Saudi Arabia through the Eyes of its Twentysomethings', Washington, DC: Wilson Center, 2013.

Niblock, Tim, *Saudi Arabia: Power, Legitimacy and Survival*, London: Routledge, 2006.

Niblock, Tim and Monica Malik, *The Political Economy of Saudi Arabia*, London: Routledge, 2007.

Ottaway, David, *The King's Messenger: Prince Bandar Bin Sultan and America's Tangled Relationship with Saudi Arabia*, New York: Walker & Company, 2008.

———— 'Saudi Arabia's Race against Time', Washington, DC: Wilson Center, Occasional Paper, Summer 2012.

al-Rasheed, Madawi, *Contesting the Saudi State: Islamic Voices from a New Generation*, Cambridge: Cambridge University Press, 2007.

———— (ed.), *Kingdom without Borders: Saudi Arabia's Political, Religious and Media Frontiers*, London: Hurst, 2008.

———— *A History of Saudi Arabia*, Cambridge: Cambridge University Press, 2002.

———— *A Most Masculine State: Gender, Politics, and Religion in Saudi Arabia*, Cambridge University Press, 2013.

Rentz, George S., *The Birth of the Islamic Reform Movement in Saudi Arabia*, London: Arabian Publishing, 2004.

Schanzer, Jonathan and Steven Miller, 'Facebook Fatwa: Saudi Clerics, Wahhabi Islam and Social Media', Washington, DC: Foundation for Defense of Democracies, 2012.

al-Shihabi, Ali, *The Saudi Kingdom: Between the Jihadi Hammer and the Iranian Anvil*, Gloucester: The Choir Press, 2015.

Stenslie, Stig, *Regime Stability in Saudi Arabia: The Challenge of Succession*, London: Routledge, 2012.

Teitelbaum, Joshua, *Holier Than Thou: Saudi Arabia's Islamic Opposition*, Washington, DC: Washington Institute for Near East Policy, 2000.

Thompson, Mark, *Saudi Arabia and the Path to Political Change: National Dialogue and Civil Society*, London: I.B. Tauris, 2014.

Trofimov, Yaroslav, *The Siege of Mecca: The Forgotten Uprising*, London: Allen Lane, 2007.

Unger, Craig, *House of Bush, House of Saud: The Secret Relationship between the World's Two Most Powerful Dynasties*, New York: Scribner, 2004.

Vasiliev, Alexei, *The History of Saudi Arabia*, London: Saqi, 2000.

Vitalis, Robert, *America's Kingdom: Mythmaking on the Saudi Oil Frontier*, Stanford, CA: Stanford University Press, 2007.

FURTHER READING

Wehrey, Frederic, 'The Forgotten Uprising in the Eastern Province', Washington, DC: Carnegie Endowment for International Peace, 2013.

Weston, Mark, *Prophets and Princes: Saudi Arabia from Muhammad to the Present*, Hoboken, NJ: John Wiley & Sons, 2008.

Wilson, Rodney, Abdullah al-Salamah, Monica Malik and Ahmed al-Rajhi, *Economic Development in Saudi Arabia*, London: Routledge Curzon, 2004.

Yamani, May, *Changed Identities: Challenge of the New Generation in Saudi Arabia*, London: Royal Institute of International Affairs, 2000.

——— *Cradle of Islam: The Hijaz and the Quest for an Arabian Identity*, London: I.B. Tauris, 2004.

INDEX

INDEX

INDEX